ABOUT CROP

CROP, the Comparative Research Programme on Poverty, is a response from the academic community to the problem of poverty. The programme was initiated in 1992, and the CROP Secretariat was officially opened in June 1993 by the director-general of UNESCO, Dr Federico Mayor.

In recent years, poverty alleviation, reduction or even eradication of poverty has moved up the international agenda, and the CROP network is providing research-based information to policy-makers and others responsible for poverty reduction. Researchers from more than 100 countries have joined the CROP network, with more than half coming from so-called developing countries and countries in transition.

The major aim of CROP is to produce sound and reliable knowledge which can serve as a basis for poverty reduction. This is done by bringing together researchers for workshops, co-ordinating research projects and publications, and offering educational courses for the international community of policy-makers.

CROP is multi-disciplinary and works as an independent non-profit organization.

For more information you may contact the CROP Secretariat:

CROP Secretariat
Fosswinckelsgate 7
N-5007 Bergen
Norway
Tel: +47-5558-9739 Fax: +47-5558-9745
E-mail: crop@uib.no
CROP on the Internet: http://www.crop.org

CROP is a programme under the International Social Science Council

CROP PUBLICATIONS

Poverty: Research Projects, Institutes, Persons, Tinka Ewoldt-Leicher and Arnaud F. Marks (eds), Tilburg, Bergen, Amsterdam, 1995, 248 pp.

Urban Poverty: Characteristics, Causes and Consequences, David Satterthwaite (ed.), special issue of *Environment and Urbanization*, Vol. 7, no. 1, April 1995, 283 pp.

Urban Poverty: From Understanding to Action, David Satterthwaite (ed.), special issue of *Environment and Urbanization*, Vol. 7, no. 1, October 1995, 283 pp.

Women and Poverty – the Feminization of Poverty, Ingrid Eide (ed.), The Norwegian National Commission for UNESCO and CROP, Oslo and Bergen (published in Norwegian only), 56 pp.

Poverty: A Global Review. Handbook on International Poverty Research, Else Øyen, S. M. Miller, Syed Abdus Samad (eds), Oslo and Paris, Scandinavian University Press and UNESCO, 1996, 620 pp.

Poverty and Participation in Civil Society, Yogesh Atal and Else Øyen (eds), Paris and New Delhi, UNESCO and Abhinav Publications, 1997, 152 pp.

Law, Power and Poverty, Asbjørn Kjønstad and John H. Veit Wilson (eds), Bergen, CROP Publications, 1997, 148 pp.

Poverty and Social Exclusion in the Mediterranean Area, Karima Korayem and Maria Petmesidou (eds), Bergen, CROP Publications, 1998, 286 pp.

Poverty and the Environment, Arild Angelsen and Matti Vainio (eds), Bergen, CROP Publications, 1998, 180 pp.

The International Glossary on Poverty, David Gordon and Paul Spicker (eds), CROP International Studies in Poverty Research, London, Zed Books, 1999, 162 pp.

Poverty and the Law, Peter Robson and Asbjørn Kjønstad (eds), Oxford, Hart Publishing, 2001, 199 pp.

Poverty Reduction: What Role for the State in Today's Globalised Economy?, Francis Wilson, Nazneen Kanji and Einar Braathen (eds), CROP International Studies in Poverty Research, London, Zed Books, 2001, 372 pp.

The Poverty of Rights – Human Rights and the Eradication of Poverty, Willem van Genugten and Camilo Perez-Bustillo (eds), CROP International Studies in Poverty Research, London, Zed Books, 2001, 209 pp.

BEST PRACTICES IN POVERTY REDUCTION
An Analytical Framework

ELSE ØYEN

In co-operation with

Alberto Cimadamore
Michel Flament Fultot
Anuradha Joshi
Joachim Hvoslef Krüger
Santosh Mehrotra
S. M. Miller
Mick Moore
Erika Vidal
Fabiana M. Werthein

CROP
International Studies in
Poverty Research

Zed Books
LONDON · NEW YORK

Best Practices in Poverty Reduction: An Analytical Framework was first published by Zed Books Ltd, 7 Cynthia Street, London N1 9JF, UK and Room 400, 175 Fifth Avenue, New York, NY 10010, USA in 2002.

www.zedbooks.demon.co.uk

CROP International Studies in Poverty Research

Cover designed by Andrew Corbett
Set in Monotype Fournier by Ewan Smith, London
Printed and bound in the United Kingdom by Biddles Ltd, Guildford and King's Lynn

Distributed in the USA exclusively by Palgrave, a division of St Martin's Press, LLC, 175 Fifth Avenue, New York, NY 10010.

A catalogue record for this book is available from the British Library

ISBN 1 84277 210 4 cased
ISBN 1 84277 211 2 limp

Contents

Preface

• The notion of 'best practices' comes from the political and administrative world of anti-poverty strategies. It is a concept that the world of research has found hard to handle because there are few relevant analytical tools available. Researchers are faced with a choice of either ignoring it or trying to make it more useful. We decided on the latter.

Those responsible for anti-poverty interventions want to learn from successful experiments elsewhere that can be transferred to their own national or cultural setting. This is a sensible approach that, with increasing globalization, will gain impetus in the years to come. However, it is also a risky approach because cultural variations as well as variations in the target groups are likely to make it difficult to transfer a successful programme directly into a different culture.

This book is an examination of the use of best practices for more efficient poverty reduction. It is also a tool to help develop a more systematic approach to the understanding of what constitutes best practice. In other words, it attempts to develop a methodology for understanding and utilizing best practices. Best practices are presented in different ways. Often they are reported as 'success stories', without specifying the criteria by which they are judged successful. Sometimes we are introduced to best practices as 'learning experiences', something worthy of being used in another setting. They also present a technical challenge: can 'best practices' be assembled in a database and offered to interested parties? While this may give impetus to new ideas, it can also be counter-productive if it ignores the social forces surrounding a practice.

This little book is a guide to the development and functioning of a best practice. It demonstrates how each is deeply embedded in the social setting in which it operates and how its success depends upon the political and moral climate of individual cultures. The challenge is to identify those specific circumstances that will make a best practice both sustainable and transferable to another setting. Three of the chapters — those by Anuradha Joshi and Mick Moore, S. M. Miller, and Santosh

Mehrotra — analyse through different perspectives the processes underlying the development of a best practice and the organizational variables influencing the transition of an ordinary practice into a best practice. They emphasize the importance of policy-making, in spite of strong social forces running counter to poverty reduction.

Other parts of the book offer concrete advice on how to evaluate best practices and how to avoid the pitfalls when they are transferred to another setting. Alberto Cimadamore et al., and Santosh Mehrotra show how to identify a best practice from among hundreds of ongoing practices. Else Øyen suggests ways to analyse practices and their impacts and how to compare them. Joachim Hvoslef Krüger presents the results of a search through different databases concerned with best practices.

Each chapter has a distinctive approach to the understanding of best practices in poverty reduction. Together they form the first attempt to take the concept of a best practice out of its politicized and practical applications and to treat it as a scientific tool in the search for an understanding of the many failures in poverty reduction. While acknowledging the obstacles to be faced when developing such a tool, it is still necessary to move forwards and to look for ways to identify, develop and promote those practices that seem to add significantly to poverty reduction.

CROP, the Comparative Research Programme on Poverty, has added other tools to the toolbox of poverty analysis. The first was an overview of poverty researchers and the institutions working within different areas of poverty research. The second was a review of the frontiers of poverty research in different regions worldwide. The third was a glossary on the many concepts of poverty that have appeared in poverty research (see 'CROP Publications', p. ii).

Best Practices in Poverty Reduction is one of the projects within CROP and it will continue beyond this publication. Workshops will be organized around certain best practices to determine which factors lead to success and which factors hinder the implementation process. As long as 'best practices' is a central strategy in poverty reduction, the concept and the results it delivers will be followed with a keen scientific eye. Early in the project, a joint CROP/MOST competition was announced, inviting the submission of papers giving a theoretical input to the understanding of the development of best practices. Chapter 2 by Joshi and Moore presented here received joint first prize, with Mohammad Shafi of Aligarh Muslim University, India, whose paper was entitled

'Best Practices in Poverty Reduction and Management of Social Transformation'.

In November 1999, a group of international scholars held a conference in Amman, Jordan, under the patronage of Her Royal Highness Princess Basma Bint Talal, to analyse the concept of best practices, bringing it into academic discussion on anti-poverty policies (see 'Participants in the Project', p. 138). They commented generously on the first draft of the chapters presented here. The conference was jointly organized by CROP and the UNESCO Amman Office.

Financial support for this project has been received from the International Social Science Council, UNESCO, the UNESCO MOST programme, the UNESCO Amman Office, the Norwegian Research Council, and the Norwegian Non-fiction Writers and Translators Association.

Colleagues and friends have been used as sounding boards in a variety of discussions on the usefulness, and uselessness, of the concept of best practices. CROP consultant Inge Tesdal has helped with the technical production of this publication and CROP assistant Joachim Hvoslef Krüger helped with the references.

We are grateful for all these intellectual, financial and technical contributions.

Else Øyen, Scientific Director of CROP

ONE

A Methodological Approach to 'Best Practices'

ELSE ØYEN

• 'Best practices' is an ambitious term and for most purposes it would be better to lower our ambitions and settle instead for 'good practices'. In the notion of *best* practices lies the expectation that an intervention has been successful according to some criteria and that it is better than something else. More often than not these criteria and comparisons are not made explicit and the success is described in political rather than analytical terms. As a result, much of the valuable information on how a best practice has come about, and how it can be replicated elsewhere, is lost. At worst, knowledge from earlier learning becomes invisible and resources become absorbed in new periods of trial and error attempting to develop another best practice.[1]

In everyday language, best practices comes across as a conglomerate of several phenomena. The term is not limited to a well-planned intervention to solve or ameliorate a social problem; best practices may be used also as a good idea, an inspiration, a discourse, a technical innovation or a new practice within a profession, to mention a few examples. As a matter of fact, it is within the last two uses of the term that most of the present literature is found (see Ch. 6).

In this chapter we shall try to reach a better understanding of what a best practice in poverty reduction is and the conditions under which it might develop. The complex realities of poverty and poverty reduction will be brought in only marginally. First, we ask what can be learned about best practices from the already existing literature on evaluation research; second, we discuss how the same practice may be judged differently at different times; third, we look at transferability and how to shift a best practice from one context to another without the loss of those elements that make it a best practice; fourth, we discuss political variables and the impact of vested interests on the outcome and judgement of best practices; fifth, we ask who are the users and who are to be the judges of whether a practice is best; finally, we examine the impact of best practices on poverty reduction and offer some directions for those who want to identify a good practice and transfer it to another setting.

BEST PRACTICES AND EVALUATION

Evaluation research analyses the effects of specific interventions; some label it applied research.[2] The types of interventions to be studied vary from a small well-defined public programme, intended to reach a small well-defined target group within a limited time, to a broad programme reaching out to a heterogeneous group of people with a multiple set of desirable and not too well-defined effects to be developed over a long period.

The more variables involved in the evaluation of an intervention, the more difficult are the methodology and the theoretical work needed. It should be stressed that evaluation procedures are only a tool for developing a more systematic understanding of how an intervention works. An evaluation procedure is not magic. Only partial information can ever be ascertained, and the border between information produced by professional evaluators and information owned by non-professional participants in the intervention is diffuse and at times difficult to penetrate.

In some ways a best practices approach can be described as an 'evaluation-light'. The language of evaluation research may be used while the strict criteria of evaluation research are transformed into a more intuitive understanding of what is successful and why. Some will argue that only professional evaluators should be allowed to judge the quality of an intervention. Others will argue that non-professional evaluators who are close to the intervention should be also included to broaden the perspective.

For professional and non-professional evaluators alike, there are certain basic criteria that can improve the quality and credibility of a best practice approach. At least five elements need to be taken into account in the process of identifying and describing the evolution of a best practice.

At the outset, it is necessary to establish a starting point for the intervention and to identify the target group. What was the situation for the group before the intervention, both in general and in terms of those specific circumstances that the intervention is designed to change? What is the problem and how can the living conditions of the target group be described? Can certain indicators of the problem be identified and can they be monitored and followed throughout the intervention? Without a baseline at the outset it is difficult to establish a convincing case of progress from an intended good intervention to a best practice. This part of the methodology can sometimes be seen in the original argument for why an intervention was needed.

A second element in this process is to describe the goals of the intervention, however diffuse they may be, and the expected results. This is not a straightforward procedure. Goals may come in clusters and become even more difficult to describe when different parts of the bureaucratic and political system define different goals or criteria for success. Miller (see Ch. 3) provides examples of layers of goals defined by different actors who have different interests in the outcome of an intervention. Unanticipated effects, both positive and negative, are likely to develop along the way, and these in turn may change the original goal(s). A study by Berner (1999) shows how public interventions designed to help squatters gain legal access to the land they occupied took a wrong turn. Grand schemes with ambitious housing projects and legal regulations increased the price of land and eventually drove out the poor. The squatters would have been better off with a step-by-step implementation process, starting with a minimal infrastructure and limited services that allowed the users to steer the process themselves. Contrary to conventional wisdom and under certain circumstances, an illegal system of taking over land may actually provide a better practice in creating housing for squatters than a legal one.

A third element is to make visible the kind of instruments for change that are built into the intervention. What kind of principles and ethical considerations does the intervention build on? What kind of expertise is needed to fulfil the goals of the intervention? How is the intervention organized and financed? Who are responsible for its implementation? What is the role of the users? What kind of resources are allocated and what guarantees are given that the financing will be continued until the intervention has achieved its goals? Built into the organization of the intervention are features that will increase or decrease the probability of the intervention ending up as a best practice. Joshi and Moore (see Ch. 2) stress the need for an intervention to be predictable for the users as well as for the other people involved. The officials in charge must establish their credibility before the users can trust them and their intentions. The intervention must be stable over time, in content and in procedures. Users must be given a formal right to benefits delivered through the programme. Joshi and Moore see these requirements as basic to the success of any anti-poverty programme.

A fourth element of significance for the evaluation is the political and cultural climate in which the intervention is launched. Are these surroundings positive or is there opposition to the intervention? From where does the support for the intervention come and who are antagonistic towards it? This is an issue that comes to the fore in interventions intended to reduce poverty. Poverty reduction is more than anything else a question of the redistribution of resources, whether it be land, water, power, or monetary, political, educational or symbol-laden resources. In essence it means that some groups have to relinquish their resources and privileges and turn them over to a group for whom they may not have much love. Poverty reduction needs to be analysed within a conflict paradigm if further understanding is to be gained (Øyen 1996).

A fifth element is discussion of the implications of different time horizons. At what point in time should the intervention be judged and defined? Why is a certain timing chosen to declare the intervention a best practice? Is it for reasons of a financial, political or professional nature? Is the money running out? Do those in charge need to show a success story? Have the original goals been achieved? What might have happened had a different timing been chosen? Is there an optimum time at which to judge the progress of a practice? Can something be termed a best practice only when it has attained its goals and thereby made itself superfluous?

The latter question stresses two features of an evaluation. One is that any intervention goes through different stages and the point in time at which the performance is judged reflects a stage rather than a final performance. The other is the dilemma posed by the starting point of the observation. When an intervention is initiated there is no way to guarantee that it will actually grow into a best practice.

The presentation above lays out some of the difficulties faced by those who engage in the evaluation of what leads to a best practice. For some of those who do not have a professional background it may sound discouraging. Others can take it as a rough guide to some of the important issues they will face when entering the field.[3]

BEST PRACTICES AS A PROCESS

A best practice in one time may not be a best, or even a good, practice in another time. What is 'best' is linked to a society's normative values about what is good and bad, and those values change. The welfare state programmes in the Nordic countries of fifty years ago would hardly be seen as adequate today. They have developed over time and the Nordic people have increased their standard of living and their expectations of the level of services that should be provided by the health-care system. At the same time, citizens of many poorer countries would welcome such outdated welfare state programmes if they were introduced in their own countries today. This example only proves that the concept of best practice is elusive and needs to be understood as a process that is tied to normative values and changes over time.

The historical development of a country provides a framework for any intervention and influences its consequent development. In the study undertaken by Mehrotra and his associates (see Ch. 4), a set of best practices is identified and the historical processes are traced to see if there are traits in the national history which led not only to increased public spending on health and education, but to an organizational form that also benefited the marginalized populations. While history cannot be changed, there is a large learning potential if crucial factors influencing the outcome of a best practice can be identified. The study challenges the widespread belief that wealth and economic growth are the most important variables in the development of mass education and reduction in child mortality and disease.[4] The historical approach used in the study is labelled 'painstaking' by the author and calls for a large team and intensive research work.

This study, and studies by Joshi and Moore (see Ch. 2), Miller (see Ch. 3) and Cimadamore et al. (see Ch. 5) all emphasize *participation* as a crucial variable in the process of an intervention becoming a 'best practice'. It is interesting to note that they focus on different kinds of participation which in turn may yield different kinds of impact on the future of a best practice. Mehrotra stresses more formal participation through democratic systems, with multi-party systems and free and fair elections. People in general, not only the poor, participate with their votes, or at least scope is given for them to add their voices to the decision-making process. Joshi and Moore point to the fact that 'even in the most participatory programmes, there is little interest in whether poor people are engaged in collective action to make demands on the state, to enforce their rights or to engage in political action for change'. The challenge is to design anti-poverty interventions in such a way that the users engage in collective action to benefit from the intervention and further improve their living conditions. Joshi and Moore emphasize the implementation phase as the most important stage in the process of an intervention. It is at that stage that the major decisions are made concerning design, organization and commitment. Once the intervention is under way it is more difficult to reorganize and increase the participation of the users. This is particularly true in poor countries due to the low level of infrastructure and formal decision-making. Miller shows in two examples how the participation of the ordinary members in a group and the absence of formal expertise contribute to the success of, respectively, a teaching programme and a voluntary organization for people with alcohol problems. Cimadamore et al. bring in the opinions of the users in their evaluation of interventions selected as candidates for best practices.

Although the results above may look contradictory, the participation of the users seems to be crucial if an intervention is to move on to become a best practice. However, it has to be the kind of participation which has a real content and the power to change the run of an intervention and influence the outcome of the process.[5]

Some interventions are launched within a harmonious atmosphere and all the major actors co-operate to secure a success. This is rarely the case with programmes aimed at efficient poverty reduction. More often than not, such programmes are launched within an atmosphere of conflicting interests. In such a context, those programmes that best fit the context survive, but they may not be the strongest or the most successful poverty-reducing programmes. Weaker programmes, with a limited impact on poverty reduction, are the ones more likely to survive because they are less challenging to their surroundings. Thus, the history of a best practice may only be the history of a second-rate practice since the best practice did not survive.

It is from this background that another crucial variable emerges. Since poverty-reducing programmes are not likely to be very popular with non-poor groups, the interventions depend on many kinds of support to survive long enough to become a best practice. Miller stresses the need for a broad *constituency* for advocacy to make a programme sustainable, while Joshi and Moore find their major constituency for the programme among the programme users.

Many of the examples of best practices have not been observed from the beginning. More often, it has been stated retrospectively that a certain intervention has actually worked, so its history has to be traced and re-created. Written records are likely to be scarce and the memories of the people involved may have faded or become influenced by later events.

Cimadamore et al. take a different approach and pitch their study at the end of the long process that leads to a best practice. They look at the here and now and ask: out of hundreds or maybe thousands of interventions how can we find those that at present are the best? They develop a method in three parts. First, they try to identify those criteria that characterize a best practice. Then they ask experts, administrators and users to identify interventions that fulfil these criteria. Finally, they move into a complex analysis that can point to a select group of best practices. The approach is innovative and systematic in the way it proceeds to locate the best practices in poverty reduction in a country, and should be developed further and tried out in several other countries. In particular, the criteria characterizing a best practice need to be scrutinized to understand better their cultural variations and how far they can be generalized to suit different kinds of practices. The preliminary results of this study are likely to become an important base for discussions on what criteria should be established in the future for successful interventions in poverty reduction.

A question of a more speculative nature is what is going to happen to a best practice once it has been declared a best practice. Is it going to be sustainable, that is, will it survive to fulfil its present functions and will it be able to adapt to future needs and changes? What are the organizational, political, economic and normative features needed to make a best practice sustainable? Miller gives an example of a *perpetuum mobile* of peer monitoring which can involve endless learning for both the mentor and the mentee. It is 'relatively inexpensive, renewable each year as a new batch of possible mentors appears for students in lower grades'. Unfortunately, few anti-poverty interventions can be expected to boast such built-in qualities. If found, they ought to be framed and hung on the wall.

There are also those best practices that have become so successful that they have fulfilled their original goals and made themselves superfluous. These are also part of the history of best practices and can provide lessons for action. The reality, however, is that programmes come and go. Most of the programmes aimed at poverty reduction never seem to live long enough to reach a stage where they can be labelled a best practice. Much of the knowledge about such failures has been lost. Paradoxical as it may sound, such knowledge is just as valuable as, or even more valuable than, the knowledge of success we are now chasing.

REPLICABILITY AND TRANSFER

It is not obvious how a best practice in one place can be replicated and transferred to another sector or country and be just as successful there. The present literature does not give an answer to how a best practice can be implanted into a new body in such a way that the patient survives. This is an area rife with trial and error.

One of the transplanted best practices cited the most often is the case of the Grameen Bank. The Grameen Bank originated in 1989 in Bangladesh and provided a credit without collateral to poor women to initiate small-scale enterprises. The women guaranteed collectively for the loan and organized repayment between them. The scheme has been a tremendous success both in terms of new initiatives, low administrative costs and a certain poverty-reducing effect.[6] The model has been implanted worldwide into so-called micro-credit schemes whereby small loans are extended to poor people for entrepreneurial activities and to help them obtain ordinary bank loans.[7] The success has been mixed, in spite of high-powered micro-credit summits with heads of state to give the scheme legitimacy. It has been a success in the sense that a micro-credit scheme like the Women's World Banking Global Network can now claim over ten million clients who would never have been welcomed by the ordinary banking system, which shuns poor customers.[8] However, the schemes have not become the expected cost-effective weapon for fighting poverty. It has been speculated that one reason is the curtailment of the '16 dogmas' built into the original Grameen scheme. These dogmas provide a set of cultural instructions linked to the use of money (for example, the loan could not be used for bridal dowry). Although the same instructions would hardly be applicable within another cultural framework, the transfer of the best practice built into the Grameen scheme became incomplete. In micro-credit schemes in other cultures a similar sort of dogma tailored to the culture was left out, perhaps because such dogmas did not have sufficient cultural impact to have an effect on the use and repayment of the loan in different cultures; or because modern economic thinking does not appreciate traditional cultural values; or because the micro-credit schemes include other and more powerful agendas than just poverty reduction.[9] As a result, the physical idea has been transferred, while some of the basic ideology has been left behind. The lesson from Bangladesh stresses the fact that an understanding of the social context is important for the successful transfer of a best practice.

The large databases on all kinds of interventions published on the Internet as 'best practices'[10] and the 'Wall on Best Practices' erected at the UN Social Summit on Development in Geneva 2000[11] ignore this principle. Rather, they present the many interventions as a bank of ideas from which anybody is invited to draw inspiration (see Ch. 6). The World Bank 'Development Marketplace' invites global competition for 'testing new approaches that will advance the fight against poverty'. The criteria for a successful approach are that the practice addresses the issue well, is innovative, gives value for money and ensures sustainability.[12] There is no discussion of the problems raised in the transfer and replicability process and what the notion of 'testing' implies. The criterion of innovation in itself defies the hard-earned learning process that goes ahead of the development of best practices in efficient poverty reduction. Also, it bars former successful practices from being brought into the marketplace of ideas, cf. for example the many successful practices of the Nordic welfare states during the last century that eradicated poverty on a large scale.

When a best practice is transferred to another culture or sector, some of the methodology from comparative studies may be mobilized (Øyen 1990 and 1992). The crucial issue is to try to develop an understanding of what it was in the original culture surrounding an intervention that promoted it into a best practice. Once this understanding has been obtained the next step is to ask (i) if the new culture or sector receiving the best practice has some of the same decisive features, and (ii) if they will actually further a successful transfer of the best practice.

This procedure is seldom done in a systematic way by people who have the necessary knowledge to judge the process of a transfer. More often the transfer starts out with a certain enthusiasm for the best practice somewhere else and it is implanted in its new environment through trial and error and adaptation. Little is known about this process. Even less systematic knowledge is available about the success or failure of the many transfers that have taken place.

Learning across borders of cultures and sectors takes place all the time, whether it is called innovation, imitation or transfer of best practices. It may be a futile exercise to follow these broader processes because so little is known about the crucial variables that affect their outcome. At the same time, unsuccessful implantations of best practices that do not obtain the desired effects, such as poverty reduction, do have a negative impact on the target group as well as on the waste of public resources. Such wastage speaks in favour of an approach that will decrease the number of unsuccessful transfers and increase the transfers of well adapted best practices.

One way to proceed is to describe the process carefully from the beginning to the point of judging a specific intervention a good, or even best, practice. The exercise is more or less the same as the one described above under the label 'evaluation light'. The same kind of understanding is needed, this time with a comparative perspective that includes both the context in which the present best practice has developed and the context into which it may become transplanted. Such a process can be carried out on several levels. Ideally it can take the form of a strict comparison, variable by variable and configuration by configuration, of phenomena considered relevant. More likely it will take the form of a 'comparative methodology light' where only certain observations are singled out for closer inspection.

One possible way to engage in such an awareness-raising exercise is to scrutinize the criteria for success. For example, did the crime rate in a certain poor neighbourhood drop as a consequence of the intervention, and if so what kind of crime and by how much did it drop? How much did it have to drop for the intervention to be defined as a success? Could the change be attributed to other kinds of phenomena occurring during the same period or to chance variations? In what context did the change take place? Was there something in the culture of the neighbourhood that increased the positive effect of the intervention? What kind of organizational set-up and choice of expertise influenced the successful outcome, and how? Were there specific cultural traits in the surrounding society that added to the success? Were there competing interventions aimed at the same target group, and if so how did these interventions affect the outcome of the best practice?

The search for causes is like the work of a detective, the description of the possible causes is like that of technician analysing a sample under an electronic microscope, and the systematizing of data is like that of a librarian putting the books on the right shelves. One may not know what one is looking for and much creative imagination is called for. The scientific control of this creativity lies in a meticulous description of the observations so others can judge their validity and relevance. When these procedures have been observed it increases the likelihood that it might be possible to state whether the results of the intervention indicate a best practice only for the specific problem to which it was tailored, or whether it is a best practice that can be tried out in a another context.

The more limited and well defined an intervention is, and the less culture-bound it is, the more manageable a transfer is likely to be. The notion of a best practice may originally have come from technology where a technical innovation such as the use of a new drill can easily be evaluated and transferred to another area. Poverty reduction is a different matter. It is a complex process and the interaction of the many variables in the process is not well known. Besides, poverty and poverty reduction are likely to be culture-bound. Much creative imagination is needed to think in comparative terms before a best practice is transferred to a new area. For those concerned with genuine poverty reduction it may be a necessary exercise. The effect of the exercise may be enhanced if participants from the host culture/sector and participants from the adopting culture/sector do the exercise together. Also, for those concerned who have limited resources the exercise seems the best route to take.

VESTED INTERESTS IN BEST PRACTICES

Success has become a symbol of the modern world and those who can report successes are rewarded. When interviewing officers at a UN organization I was told they were discouraged from reporting failures to headquarters; it would go on their personal files and reflect negatively on their future careers. Some avoided this difficult situation by not reporting at all on an unsuccessful intervention, while others would redefine the outcome and present an enhanced result. The organization needed a display of 'best practices' to convince donors. This story is not unique. A display of best practices increases favourably the image of politicians and the bureaucracy and can be used to increase the flow of goodwill and money in many organizations. Research literature on social administration, for example, has several studies that show how organizations redefine the composition of their clientele and focus on easier problems, which they can solve and display as successes, rather than face difficult problems with the hard-core clientele.

The call for increased stringency, systematization of data and documentation in the process leading to a 'best practices' approach serves another purpose besides the methodological considerations outlined above. Not only do such techniques help to screen low-quality presentations of best practices, they are also helpful in identifying some of the many internal and external interests vested in the process which leads to the implementation and outcome of what is later termed a best practice.

During the past couple of decades a major part of poverty-reducing interventions in poor countries has been donor driven. Donors have provided the moral basis for organizational and financial arrangements and flag expectations that some form of best practice should emerge. It has not been easy to implement donor-initiated interventions, for many reasons, and donors are in constant search for partners who can help deliver their initiatives in an acceptable form. In countries where the state is weak, corrupt or lacks the infrastructure to carry out pro-poor policies, donors have turned to civil society to implement poverty-reducing strategies. That is a strategy with many implications, including the sudden growth of seemingly best practices.

Donors need best practices to invest their funds prudently. The NGOs need best practices to legitimate or fund their activities. The political agenda needs best practices to increase donor funding and increase its standing in the global arena. The consultants who move rapidly around in the lush economic market created by the donors need best practices to show their worth and repeat their performance. The price tag for worst practices is not of interest in that market.

There is good reason to be cautious when such powerful interests coincide and become vested in the presentation of a best practice. Those who can display a best practice command at the same time a valuable political symbol and a highly priced commodity. For some it must be a temptation to deliver a product where little time has been devoted to stringency, systematization and documentation. As a result, low-quality products enter the literature on best practices without much control since donors and users alike often lack the expertise with which to judge the quality of the product.

To complicate matters further, the vested interest in the presentation of a best practice may not be the same as the vested interest in the actual outcome of a best practice. All kinds of poverty reduction, small or comprehensive, have an impact on non-poor people, whether it be in financial or political terms, or simply in symbolic terms. Some of these non-poor people will resist changes brought about by poverty-reducing interventions. At times they will have a strong vested interest in keeping poverty reduction and transfer of resources to the poor to a minimum (Gans 1973). These forces have kept the poor down for centuries and there is little indication the picture has changed. The same forces are likely to influence which interventions can be initiated and how far a best practice can develop.

In Chapter 3 Miller discusses the need to create a constituency around an intervention that will protect it from being changed, limited or even destroyed by vested interests. If poverty reduction is to be successfully turned into a best practice it needs a positive social atmosphere to protect it (or, in Bismarckian time, an authoritarian decree) and forceful groups among the non-poor to promote it. Humanitarian groups, political parties, ideological societies and committed individuals have played that role since the French Revolution. At no time have efficient poverty-reducing measures come about without resistance from vested interest groups. History, including modern history, bears witness to these conflicts. The new notion of 'partnership' between poor and non-poor groups acknowledges the need to involve powerful non-poor groups such as the business community and community leaders in a joint effort to promote poverty-reducing interventions. However, the idea of partnership is presented within a model of harmony, as if the non-poor had the same interest in poverty reduction as the poor. The notion of vested interests and conflict of interests is played down in an attempt to be diplomatic. As a result the actual conflicts of interest are made invisible and left out in the difficult negotiations to create efficient poverty reduction.[13]

So far much of the discussion on obstacles to efficient poverty reduction has been concerned with the lack of available resources. While this is certainly true, attention also needs to be paid to the many interests vested in the outcome, or lack of such, in poverty reduction and the sustainable success of best practices. In order to develop efficient poverty-reducing measures it is necessary to understand those forces that see poverty reduction as a threat to their interests. Strategies to block a poverty-reducing intervention are very often more powerful than new initiatives to reduce poverty. It means among other things that strategies to counteract those who fight for their vested interests may be just as necessary as actual poverty-reducing strategies.

WHO SHOULD BE THE JUDGES OF A BEST PRACTICE?

Against whose norms should a practice be judged 'best'? Ideally it should be the users who make this judgement. They are the ones who have to live with the consequences of a particular intervention and they are the ones who know their own needs. In practice the normative underpinnings of an intervention are derived from the administrators of the intervention, the financing agencies, the ideologists behind the origin of the intervention and other bodies who have a certain interest in the outcome of the intervention.

Much depends on who consider themselves the 'owners' of the intervention. Some interventions, although still a minority, are created in symmetrical co-operation between users and providers of administrative expertise and financing agencies. Within this model the users can voice their opinion on the functioning of the intervention with the knowledge that their opinion has an impact on the future course of the intervention. The users have the right to define the criteria for what is 'best' and whether the practice meets their expectations.

From a democratic point of view this is the ideal model. From a more future-oriented point of view the model is limited. Many of the poorest users do not have the knowledge to see their life situation within a larger setting and have a tendency to ask too little really to improve their life situation and the future of their children. In principle they have been given the ownership of the intervention and the right to use their own norms to define what is 'best'. In reality their criteria do not help make them full citizens.

The tradition has been that those who foot the bill are also the ones to set the criteria for what an intervention should achieve in order to be successful. Their norms have moral superiority and are accepted as such. The newer development is that 'experts' on poverty and organizational issues have been given space to define criteria for a successful intervention. Administrators are then delegated to execute the intervention according to these criteria. However, in practice it turns out that even the most faithful of bureaucrats will, over time, also apply their own criteria for success in order to fit their comprehension of what the intervention ought to achieve or is able to achieve. Those kinds of adaptations happen all the time and are necessary for the bureaucracy to survive. Along the way all kinds of vested interests also try to impose their norms for what should be considered the right kind of criteria for the intervention.

It is this competing conglomerate of norms and pressures that need to be taken into account when a certain intervention is presented as a 'best' practice. In terms of efficient poverty reduction, it may not be such a good practice after all, while other practices that deserve the label 'good practice' or even 'best practice' may disappear in the maze of conflicting ideas about what is 'best' for whom.

In the chapter by Cimadamore et al. an attempt is made to incorporate several of these interests when judging an intervention a best practice. The researchers have developed an index based on criteria from practitioners, administrators, users and a major organization (MOST) that has tried to systematize a set of criteria needed to judge whether an intervention can be classified as a best practice.

MOST (Management of Social Transformations, a programme under UNESCO) brings forward thirteen kinds of criteria for an intervention to be classified as a best practice. They are the ones used in the study mentioned above. The emphasis is partly on the characteristics of the intervention, such as innovative aspects, sustainability, positive impact on the target group and potential for replication; it is partly on the characteristics of the organization involved with the intervention, such as efficacy, efficiency, organizational co-operation, political viability and the participation of beneficiaries – good management is the key concept here; and it is partly on the beneficiaries' perception of the intervention, such as their view on efficacy and their own impact on the intervention. At a later stage the MOST databank adds still another criterion: best practices 'are typically based on the co-operation between national or local authorities, non-governmental organisations (NGOs) and local communities, the private sector, and academic communities'.[14] It is difficult to understand the role of this last criterion. Rather, it might be read as a message directed to parties who are invited to make use of the databank. It can hardly be considered a viable criterion for a best practice.

One of the major actors in the poverty discourse during the last decade is the World Bank. As mentioned above, the Bank has for the second time called for a worldwide competition to identify new approaches that will advance the fight against poverty. These 'best ideas' are identified as 'empowering people to participate in development and investing in them; building a better climate for investment and jobs, and sustainable growth'.[15] A further elaboration of the criteria for a best practice is given through a quotation from one of the judges of the competition who maintains that the competition looks for 'developing new products and for providing services in a more cost-effective manner, for finding new ways to do business, or simply for demonstrating a new way of working partnership'.[16] The Bank criteria for 'best' are clearly located within the Bank's major ideology of economic growth and the belief that poverty reduction lies in increased small-scale production. The criterion of sustainable growth presented cannot be operationalized into any concrete criteria that can be judged fairly by a committee. It can be seen mainly as part of the rhetoric the Bank uses throughout its documents. The last criterion, that of a working partnership, is of a somewhat different character. It points to a wider understanding of poverty reduction and the discussion introduced above on the need to create a favourable climate around a poverty-reducing intervention if it is to become a best practice. In the Bank's programme Poverty Reduction Strategy Papers (PRSPs) workshops are organized that promote 'interaction and exchange of best practices'.[17] These PRSP programmes are likely to become one of the Bank's flagships in the next few years. To the extent that best practices are defined within the programme, the definitions are dominated by economic considerations.

The United Nations Centre for Human Settlements (UNCHS) Habitat has developed a Best Practices Database after a competition inviting submissions worldwide. It states that the 'database contains over 1100 proven solutions from more than 120 countries to the common social, economic and environmental problems of an urbanising world. It demonstrates the practical ways in which communities, governments and the private sector are working together to improve governance, eradicate poverty, provide access to shelter, land and basic services, protect the environment and support economic development'.[18] In 2000 more than 700 new submissions from about 100 countries were offered (see also Ch. 6). In reaching its conclusions, the jury for the competition used 'tangible impact, partnership, and sustainability' as criteria. Furthermore, the jury gave due recognition to 'leadership, the empowerment of people and their communities, and the promotion of gender equality and of social inclusion'. Also, among the entries the jury looked for 'effective responses to emerging issues and trends brought about by the challenges of globalisation and its influences on social change' and ' gave emphasis to the interdependencies of these issues with those of human rights, good governance and the empowerment of people'. The jury recommends 'the widest possible dissemination of Best Practices' and 'encourages all partners and relevant institutions in all sectors, to actively participate in, and contribute to the Best Practice'. These criteria have developed in the years since the UNCHS database was first created and just about any intervention or project has been accepted as a best practice and included in the database. There is no discussion of what 'proven solutions' or best practices mean. The poverty-reducing criteria disappear in a mass of competing criteria. It is as if poverty reduction as a goal in itself is not enough. However, in the course of the jury decision-making, a set of ideological elements focused attention on what a best practice ought to be. The criteria are not concrete enough to be useful as more than normative guidelines. The real impact of the competition lies in the positive attitudes towards underprivileged people signalled by the jury and those behind the competition. Although the database has a misleading name, the ideology is clearly in favour of pro-poor policies.

Experts on poverty and poverty reduction represent another set of judges trying to make an impact with their criteria on what constitutes an efficient poverty-reducing strategy. Experts working on the micro-level are likely to emphasize those strategies that directly affect poverty in the community. As such, their criteria for a best practice are more likely to be in tune with the users. Experts on the macro-level are likely to emphasize national or even supranational goals and the long-term reduction of poverty; as such, they are removed from the predominant norms among users.

In tune with present thinking, there is often a call for an evaluation of the functioning and outcome of interventions. This is a procedure that gives the experts an opportunity to define the criteria for a best practice. As might be expected, the experts make use of the professional and normative framework of the background in which they were trained, whether they are economists, anthropologists or something else. It is seldom the users who ask for an evaluation. Their calls for change or for the monitoring of an intervention taking the wrong course are likely to travel through informal channels of communication only. More often it is the 'real' owners of the interventions who want to know the return on their investments in terms of increased poverty reduction or the proper use of money. The tendency in evaluations is to narrow down the indicators of a best practice to those that can be measured and compared over time. The choice of indicators can, at times, say more about the evaluators than about the intervention to be evaluated. The experts have the power, or are given the power, to define what is 'best'. At the same time it should not be forgotten that such evaluations make the criteria for a best practice more visible and lay them open for a public debate that may increase the likelihood of a practice developing into a best practice.

The notion of ownership of a practice has recently been brought out in another context. When the UNDP launched its new publication on Poverty Strategies Initiatives (2001), there was a major discussion on the need to create national ownership of the interventions. Donors were to let go of former conditionalities and leave decisions concerning organization, implementation and goals for poverty-reducing programmes to the countries receiving foreign aid. In the future the receivers themselves are to judge what are the 'best' means to obtain poverty reduction. Ideologically it seems to be the right position to take. However, it can also be argued that the donors wash their hands and forward the problems to a maze of different levels of decision-making and vested interests. National ownership may not reduce basic poverty any further; at least not in the short run. In the long run it may be the only way to go. It is interesting to note that the UNDP, which commands only limited funds, is willing to let go control over its resources. The World Bank on the other hand talks about empowerment of the poor but does not discuss national ownership or other measures that will give the Bank less control over its comprehensive resources.

The right to judge what is 'best' for millions of poor people carries with it ethical dilemmas and problems that so far have not been well exposed. Who has the legitimate right to judge what is right for others, for example, and who extends that legitimacy? Who has the right to pass judgements that serve only his/her own interests? What are the consequences of some people rather than others using their norms to make a judgement? It is important to address these questions when we know that in reality, deep down, a limited judgement of 'best' for some can mean that other people are sentenced to a continued life in poverty, or at worst their children are sentenced to dying in early childhood. Non-interference in problems of that magnitude is likely to raise even more ethical issues than interference through interventions meant to reduce poverty.

BEST PRACTICES AS A LIMITED POVERTY-REDUCING MEASURE

Poverty is a very complex phenomenon and it takes complex interventions to achieve efficient poverty reduction. One single best practice, however comprehensive, is likely to make only a dent in those regions where poverty is deep. If any kind of sizeable poverty reduction is the goal, one of the basic lessons is the need for a diversity of poverty-reducing measures directed at the same population and organized in such a way that the interventions work in tandem and reinforce each other. In his discussion of successes in anti-poverty measures, Lipton gives an array of examples from different countries that demonstrate the power of co-ordinated practices in what he terms 'the principle of joint requirements' (Lipton et al. 1998: 4). A best practice may be successful within its own limited scope, but unless it forms part of a larger picture on how to reduce long-term poverty, it is only a best practice with a moderate impact.

There is a widespread need to think in larger terms and to develop a vision in which the different best practices are but a step towards fulfilling that vision. The current trend to display large databases with hundreds of entries and organize worldwide competitions to call for still more examples of best practices creates further fragmentation. The challenge is not to show an ever-increasing number of case histories that may or may not constitute best practices; success cannot be counted in sheer numbers. The challenge is to develop a framework around these many ideas that integrates them into a larger framework towards an efficient poverty-reducing plan that incorporates all poor people in a country.

Poverty eradication, not only poverty reduction, seems to be a key concept in the many practices presented. The truth is that nothing in a single best practice can possibly lead to poverty eradication in the true sense of the term. The ruling step-by-step model that sees a few best practices as the initial stage, followed by some other good practices towards a final stage of complete poverty eradication, needs to be challenged. It needs to be clarified and defended by those who promote it. So far the model has not been spelled out theoretically and it suffers from the same shortcomings as the trickle-down model that used to be a core element in legitimating economic growth. The actual link between the different steps needs to be discussed, the ordering of the interventions and the expected progress of the process need to be outlined, and the principles of prioritizing the targets need to be made visible and inserted logically into the model. On intellectual grounds, the model is hard to defend.

It is easy to understand why the step-by-step model for best practices is favoured on political grounds. The model calls for only limited reallocation of resources and restricted intervention, and as such it diminishes the potential for conflict. We should be aware also that the step-by-step model has its ethical flaws. Not only does it favour certain categories of poor people, at the same time it excludes certain groups of poor people over an unknown period of time, maybe for lifetime.

Poverty eradication, in the wide understanding of the term, ought to be moved into the arena of more general politics. More often this responsibility is turned over to the bureaucrats or the NGOs. Both of these deal with their own limited area of responsibility and promote only those best practices that lie within their expertise or interest. As a result fragmentation increases while co-ordination is given low priority.

The good news is that many countries are now encouraged to develop pro-poor plans. Guidelines are being offered from donors, UNDP, the World Bank and different interest groups. One of the many challenges is to integrate the most successful practices already in existence in the overall plan and to develop a joint focus that enforces them mutually. Another challenge is to look beyond the many best practices and good advice of interest groups and search for more fundamental approaches. The framework surrounding human rights is one such lead. A best practice can, or should ideally, be defined as an efficient anti-poverty programme that incorporates all aspects of the UN Declaration of Human Rights of 1948, the UN Convention on the Rights of the Child of 1989, the ILO Declaration on Fundamental Principles and Rights of Work and all the other covenants and international agreements that are intended to protect human beings against violations and sub-human conditions (Van Genugten and Perez-Bustillo 2001). There is little in the mass of best practices that comes even close to such a definition. The implementation of citizenship and the role of the state in caring for all its citizens may be another lead, in spite of limited public resources (Wilson et al. 2001). The rights-oriented universal approach of the well-developed welfare states and the need to develop an inclusive vision before economic growth and an accumulated public surplus, not after, may also be a lead (Øyen 1997). Instead of developing still more free-standing best practices, the normative basis for a practice can be attached to such frameworks and the notion of 'best' be judged according to the norms within such a framework rather than left to self-appointed owners of a practice or vested interest groups.

An issue often raised is whether it is possible to create global criteria for poverty reduction. While it may be futile to develop global strategies for poverty reduction, such as for example the strategies embedded in economic growth, it may still be possible to obtain a broad global acceptance of the kind of sub-human conditions that no human being should be forced to live under. Slavery was abandoned through massive mobilization and is no longer accepted globally, although many people are still forced to live like slaves. Poverty is a modern form of slavery in which millions of people subsist on a minimum and have no control over their own lives. Faced with problems of such magnitude it can be asked if any of the many best practices presented, or even the sum of all those practices, are tailored to cope with such a challenge.

WHAT IS A BEST PRACTICE FOR POVERTY REDUCTION?

The answer is simple: a best practice is an intervention that reduces poverty. An intervention that reduces the worst kind of poverty to a sizeable degree is an even better candidate for a best practice. An intervention that keeps the gained poverty reduction at bay and ensures that none of the formerly poor slips back into poverty again is a still better candidate for a best practice. An intervention that manages to reduce several kinds of poverty rather than just one component in the complex pattern of poverty production, is a leading candidate for a best practice.

These criteria are the essence of a best practice. However, this fact is often lost in a myriad of other criteria and interests that take precedence. While some of those criteria may also be important, nothing is as important for a practice that aims at poverty reduction than just that: the reduction of the number of poor people living in sub-human conditions.

The dilemma occurs when limited resources force a choice between different kinds of poverty reduction. Should short-term and immediate poverty reduction be favoured over long-term investment in human capital formation? Is the building of a new school more important than a new well, or is inoculation against tuberculosis more important than participatory measures to increase democracy? The choices are many, and often restricted by competing interests. Educational experts will push for schools, health personnel will prioritize preventive health measures, NGOs with a participatory approach will want to invest in measures leading to more democracy, and interest groups will bring forward their special understanding of what is needed in poverty reduction. All will speak warmly in favour of their own strategy. Since there exists no scientifically based method to decide if one kind of intervention leads faster to comprehensive poverty reduction than another, the decision-making field is open to many interested players. The methodological challenge is how to measure and compare the amount of poverty reduced through different interventions.

How much poverty reduction is sufficient for people to claim that an intervention has been successful and should be classified as a best practice? Some countries have tried to solve this problem by establishing a poverty line or certain educational or housing standards under which no citizen should fall. Most best practices as outlined in the present databases (see also Ch. 6) do not operate with certain goals for poverty reduction to be filled. They just tell us that their interventions work, and even work well. Actual figures for how much poverty reduction has been achieved are usually absent, or we are presented with figures that make little sense. One of the examples shown is that of an Indian bank that provides credit at reasonable rates to self-employed women workers. A measure of success presented is that the bank now has assets worth USD 6.6 million.[19] It is not clear why this figure is essential for poverty reduction and we are not told how these assets are invested.

When judging a candidate for a best practice it is not sufficient to say that poverty reduction has taken place. No practice can be considered best unless it is accompanied by a trustworthy monitoring system that gives a reliable picture of how much poverty reduction has been obtained through a certain intervention.

One of the often-repeated criteria for a best practice in poverty reduction is that it should demonstrate efficiency and efficacy. Phrased in simpler terms it can be taken to mean that available resources should be used carefully and cost-effectively. This is a sound principle of good management that ought to follow all interventions financed by public (and private) means. Nothing is new here. But why are these criteria linked so closely to poverty-reducing interventions and what is their specific connection to poverty reduction? Is it due to a built-in fear of misuse by the poor? Is there an expectation of squandering money in favour of the poor? Is it due to an observation that many of those who are given responsibility for poverty-reducing interventions are appointed from among the less qualified part of the bureaucracy and so need to be better controlled?

Another criterion often put forward for a best practice in poverty reduction is that it should be sustainable. In some ways it can be said that sustainability in poverty reduction is a contradiction in terms. Sustainability presupposes that poverty is an infinite problem that needs interventions that go on and on. At the same time, poverty reduction is supposed to do away with poverty up to a certain level, that is, the success of a best practice is to make itself superfluous, not to be sustained. Therefore, it should rather be stressed that the *results* of the interventions should be sustainable, not necessarily the intervention as such. An intervention could hardly be termed a best practice if it needs to go on for ever in order to have an effect.

At this stage it is necessary to distinguish between sustainability needed for the kind of poverty that builds on still new cohorts of deprived people and the kind of poverty reduction needed for a stable population of poor people. The educational system, for example, needs to be sustainable because still new cohorts of students need it. Other poverty-reducing interventions need to be so flexible that sustainability will hamper their success and their ability to reduce poverty further. They need to change their goals and organizational structure as they reach their original goals. This is another of the many paradoxes built into poverty reduction. On the one hand an organization needs stability and predictability in order to be effective and to create trust among the beneficiaries and the surroundings. On the other hand the organization needs sufficient manoeuvring space to meet the complexity of problems inherent in poverty and the ability to move on when one kind of poverty has been sufficiently reduced or even eliminated.

The issues outlined above demonstrate the care that should be taken when transferring a concept from one arena to another. Sustainability has its roots in the environmental arena, and although disputed still reflects both a methodological and ideological approach that is considered useful. It is not as easy to see its usefulness as a vital and indisputable criterion for a best practice.

Should a best practice always work within a democratic setting? A criterion often repeated is that an intervention should be based on shared decision-making and the participation of the beneficiaries and the surrounding community. The expectation is that over time a so-called participatory intervention will lead to the increased participation of the marginalized in political life in general as well as to a wide democratization of the country. The principle can be defended on ethical grounds and within the framework of long-term poverty reduction. Still, several critical voices have been raised on this account. One is methodological. The explicit links between an intervention and a broader participation in democratic life by the poor need to be spelled out and documented. So far the reasoning has been mainly of an ideological nature. It is assumed that participation in a community project over time will educate poor people to be part of democratic decision-making also on a broader scale. That may be true. But it is necessary also to take into account that poor people are marginalized in many other parts of society. Even well-established democracies such as the United States have not found a way of making homeless and poor people part of the democratic institutions; in the US poor people do not vote or make their voices heard. Another objection raised is that efficient democracy-building needs to find other outlets and not be mixed up with poverty-reducing interventions. Poverty reduction is a project of its own and so important that it should not be slowed down by other considerations, whether they be democracy building, the preservation of indigenous cultures or other important issues not directly related to immediate poverty reduction. It can be argued that a benevolent dictator might obtain as much poverty reduction through an intervention without democracy as a western beneficiary with woolly expectations of the broad participation of all parties involved (cf. the Age of the Enlightened Despot). Still another objection has been raised on the grounds that democracy has its roots in the western culture and does not necessarily suit a local community, or country for that matter, in the South. Donors are mostly from the West and the tendency is to make democratic measures part of their conditions for giving aid.

A practice is not an isolated phenomenon; it is created within a context that over time will make it grow or wither. Most practices that aim at poverty reduction are likely to be vulnerable at the outset. The chances of survival are slim if the surrounding culture is negative. Actually, it looks as though a practice can become best only if it has a best context.

A practice needs backing by people who are willing to protect and defend it and, it should be added, are in position where their protection has an impact. Motives for defending a poverty-reducing intervention may not be relevant. Devotion to a certain cause, fear of contagion, display of expertise, political opportunism and sheer humanism are forces that may unite in defence of the intervention.

Where the surrounding culture is hostile to a certain kind of poverty reduction, it is less likely that a reducing effect will take place. And as we well know, efficient poverty-reducing strategies, not just symbolic practices with limited impact, are more than likely to meet opposition. The more effective they may become and the more built-in redistributive effect they have, the more resistance they are likely to meet. Little is known about how many potential best practices have petered out at an early stage due to a hostile context.

For those who initiate a new practice aimed at poverty reduction it is imperative to take into account those destructive forces. They need to be identified, and strategies to control vested interests ought to be part of the overall strategy for establishing a new practice. However, the control of such interests is usually located in arenas different from those where poverty-reducing strategies belong and is not seen as part and parcel of the same problem. Donors have come from the outside and have suffered from that experience, as have bureaucrats coming from the inside.

Much of the resistance to poverty-reducing practices is due not only to the antagonists' self-interest and the potential loss they may have from redistributive measures; much of their hostility stems from lack of concrete knowledge about poor people and the causes and consequences of poverty. Negative stereotypes about poverty flourish and creep into our images of who the poor people are and how their behaviour can be interpreted as asocial and deviant. An ideal best practice ought to have a pedagogical element that could impact positively on the surrounding culture and help change the ruling negative stereotypes. The non-poor need to be educated if poverty-reducing strategies are to work according to the intentions.

In order to understand better how to create successful practices we need to learn more not only about the history of successful practices and the contexts that shaped them; we also need to know more about unsuccessful practices and the contexts that stopped them or transformed them into inefficient poverty-reducing strategies. Actually, there is a need for a database on all those practices that failed and why they failed. The learning potential from that kind of knowledge is as important as the knowledge derived from successful practices.

There are millions of practices out there. Some of them end up in a database and are called best practices. Other practices are less formalized and simply work, and work well, such as traditional ways of coping and redistributing surplus according to need. The anthropologists have given us many examples of how the surplus of a sudden catch of fish is distributed in the local community or how the extended family takes responsibility for its members in times of distress. Even much despised corruption may help to keep poverty at bay in an extended family. Voluntary organizations of many kinds flourish and reach out to poor people. Some make it into the databases, others not. International organizations like the Red Crescent and the Red Cross make invaluable contributions to poverty reduction without being visible in the discussion on best practices. The field is heterogeneous and no system has been established to decide what should be named a practice for poverty reduction. Some fish are caught in a net that has been cast widely. But the reality is that the lack of a precise definition of a 'best practice' leaves us without a tool to sort out and better understand the complexity of all those efforts that appear under the name of best practices.

NOTES

I want to thank the participants in the CROP/ISSC/MOST workshop on 'best practices' and Professor Francis Wilson, University of Cape Town, for valuable comments.

1. The notion of 'practice' is likewise ambiguous. It points to something smaller than a social policy or an anti-poverty programme, it hints at something which has been practised and thus has a history, and it incorporates the traditions of medical and quasi-medical professions that carry out a professional and recognized activity. A 'practice' is a non-threatening concept, while a 'pro-poor intervention' or a 'policy to reduce poverty' carries a more powerful message, in particular when linked to the word 'best'.

2. The relationship between general social science research and evaluation research is close, in so far as they follow the same scientific rules and often target the same social areas. Usually, evaluation research has a more narrow focus.

3. Any good introductory textbook in evaluation research can take the reader further on these issues. See for example Feinstein and Picciotto (2000); Guba and Lincoln (1995); Mohr (1995); Posavac and Garey (1989); European Commission (1999).

4. See for example World Bank (2000). For a more nuanced discussion see Lipton et al. (1998).

5. This mode of thinking leads to the discussion of whether the poor are the 'experts on poverty', as argued in the April draft of the *World Development Report* World Bank (2000). While it can easily be agreed that the poor are experts on their own problems, it can also be argued that a major part of their problems is created outside their world and as such is 'invisible' to the poor. In this discussion it is crucial to make clear on which level the argument takes place.

6. For more information about the Grameen Bank see www.grameen-info.org

7. www.microcreditsummit.org/newsletter/best.htm and the Virtual Library on Microcredit.

8. Nancy Barry, 'Building Financial Systems that Work for the Majority in Middle Income Countries', paper presented at the Dräger Foundation conference on poverty in middle-income countries, Lübeck, June 2001.

9. See for example ibid.

10. UNCHS-Habitat Best Practice database; UNESCO MOST database at www.unesco.org/most/bpindi.htm, see also Ch. 6.

11. Also called 'Wall of Transformation for the Eradication of Poverty'. NGOs were invited to buy a brick at USD50 and place it on the wall with their best practice written on it. Responsible was the CONGO Facilitating Committee Working Group 'Best Practices'.

12. www.developmentmarketplace.org/html/evalcriteria.html

13. See for example World Bank (2000).

14. 2 June 2001, www.unesco.org/most/bphome.htm

15. 26 March 2001, www.developmentmarketplace.org/html/evalcriteria.html

16. Ibid.

17. 2 June 2001, www.worldbank.org/poverty/strategies/events/

18. 2 June 2001, www.bestpractices.org/

19. The Shri Mahila SEWA Sahakari Bank, figure quoted in MOST Clearing House Best Practices database, www.unesco.org/most/bphome-htm, June 2001.

REFERENCES

Berner, Erhard (1999) 'Learning from Informal Markets: Innovative Approaches to Land and Housing', paper presented at CROP/ISSC/UNESCO/MOST workshop on 'Best Practices in Poverty Reduction', Amman, Jordan, November 1999.

Environment & Urbanization (2001) 'Rethinking Aid to Urban Poverty Reduction: Lessons for Donors', Vol. 1, no. 1 (available on-line).

European Commission (1999) DG XVI; EC Structural Funds, *Evaluating Socio-*

economic Programmes, Vols 1–3 (Luxembourg: Office for Official Publications of the European Communities).

Feinstein, Osvaldo and Robert Picciotto (eds) (2000) *Evaluation and Poverty Reduction: Proceedings from a World Bank Conference* (Washington DC: World Bank).

Gans, Herbert J. (1973) 'The Positive Functions of Poverty', *American Journal of Sociology*, Vol. 78, no. 2.

Grinspun, Alejandro (ed.) (2001) *Choices for the Poor: Lessons from National Poverty Strategies* (New York: UNDP).

Guba, Egon G. and Yvonna S. Lincoln (1995) *Fourth Generation Evaluation* (Newbury Park, CA: Sage Publications).

International Fund for Agricultural Development (IFAD) (2001) *Rural Poverty Report 2001: The Challenge of Ending Rural Poverty* (Oxford: Oxford University Press).

Lipton, Michael et al. (1998) *Successes in Anti-poverty* (Geneva: International Labour Office).

Mohr, Lawrence B. (1995) *Impact Analysis for Program Evaluation* (Thousand Oaks, CA: Sage Publications).

Øyen, Else (1992) 'Some Basic Issues in Comparative Poverty Research', *International Social Science Journal*, no. 134, pp. 615–26.

— (1996) 'Poverty Research Rethought', in Else Øyen, S. M. Miller and Syed Abdus Samad (eds), *Poverty: A Global Review. Handbook in International Poverty Research* (Oslo and Paris: Scandinavian University Press and UNESCO).

— (1997) 'Some Basic Welfare Measures for Combating Poverty. Lessons from a Formerly Poor Country', in *Poverty and Plenty. The Botswana Experience* (Gaborone: Botswana Society).

Øyen, Else (ed.) (1990) *Comparative Methodology. Theory and Practice in International Social Research* (London: Sage Publications).

Posavac, Emil J. and Raymond G. Garey (1989) *Program Evaluation: Methods and Case Studies* (Englewood Cliffs, NJ: Prentice Hall).

Van Genugten, Willem and Camilo Perez-Bustillo (eds) (2001) *The Poverty of Rights. Human Rights and the Eradication of Poverty*, CROP International Studies in Poverty Research (London and New York: Zed Books).

Wilson, Francis, Nazneen Kanji and Einar Braathen (eds) (2001) *Poverty Reduction. What Role for the State in Today's Globalized Economy?* CROP International Studies in Poverty Research (London and New York: Zed Books).

World Bank (2000) *World Development Report 2000–2001: Attacking Poverty* (Oxford: Oxford University Press).

TWO

Enabling Environments and Effective Anti-poverty Programmes

ANURADHA JOSHI AND MICK MOORE

• Dealing with poverty in developing countries has become a matter of some political priority for the international community. With the adoption of the poverty targets in the OECD countries and the focus of the 2001 *World Development Report on Poverty*, there is now a climate in which new approaches to the problem of poverty are called for. The so-called New Poverty Agenda set by the World Bank in the *1990 World Development Report* no longer represents orthodoxy. That is a positive change, for the New Poverty Agenda has in practice provided licence for governments to turn away from poverty concerns. It is not that the core components of the New Agenda – 'pro-poor growth', better public services for the poor, and 'safety nets' (only) for those who really need them – are intellectually indefensible. In an era of tight fiscal constraints, one can make a convincing case for the priorities that it establishes. The problem lies rather in the implicit messages: that measures directly to combat poverty are not of prime concern; and that priority should go to promoting 'pro-poor growth', despite ignorance about how to do this.

There is now scope to argue for real priority for poverty through direct public action, without being on the intellectual defensive. What can we make of the opportunity? It is not sufficient just to ask that more public money and other resources be devoted to poverty alleviation. We cannot ignore the partial validity of the neo-liberal critique of public action: intentions and outcomes are different; public programmes intended to benefit the poor often leak into the pockets of the non-poor, who are more organized, articulate and informed (World Bank 1997: ch. 3). It is important that public resources be better used. Given the opportunity presented by the current climate, can we offer new ideas for planning and implementing anti-poverty programmes?

One way of approaching the question is to search for 'best practices', programmes that have found effective ways of reducing poverty through specific strategies. This approach involves defining success in anti-poverty programmes, analysing successful programmes to understand what made them successful and then using these effective mechanisms or 'best practices' to identify successful strategies elsewhere. Our approach to the question is somewhat broader – in this chapter we attempt to identify a set of characteristics common to anti-poverty programmes deemed to be effective. Thus the focus is not on the best practice in a particular type of programme – such as micro-credit or preventive health – but to look for generic features across programmes that have made them work better than others.

We argue this approach through several steps. There is a generic problem in anti-poverty interventions: the intended recipients, the poor, tend to be politically weak, in the broad sense of that term, in relation to public agencies and the non-poor. Anti-poverty interventions in poor countries will tend to work better if the intended recipients can increase their influence over the implementation stages through collective action of various kinds. How can that be achieved? The focus of this chapter is on one path: the role of anti-poverty interventions themselves in mobilizing their clients. We argue that anti-poverty programmes may, and should, be designed and managed such that they either (i) positively stimulate among the intended recipients the collective action that is needed to make the programmes more effective or (ii), less ambitious, at least do not discourage and frustrate collective action. We advance a conceptual framework to help us think more constructively about the conditions under which public anti-poverty interventions might result in positive consequences.

First we locate the arguments of this paper in a theoretical context and next provide details on why the implementation stage of the public policy process is so important from the perspective of poverty interventions. Our main conceptual framework is then laid out: the overarching concept of *predictability*, with three sub-categories – *credibility*, *programme stability* and *formal entitlement*. We illustrate the usefulness of these concepts through two case studies. The following section deals with the contribution of credibility to the success of a programme that requires what we have called a *concordant* relationship between groups of poor people and external agencies. Next we explore the ways in which pro-gramme stability and formal entitlement have brought considerable benefits to the poor through a programme that has involved them in relationships with government agencies that are frequently *discordant*. Through a review of recent trends in anti-poverty interventions, the case is made that the issues we have discussed under the term *predictability* are widely ignored in the practice of anti-poverty interventions.

PREDICTABILITY IN THEORETICAL CONTEXT

There are two main sources of theoretical inspiration behind this chapter. The first is a set of questions about the management of dev-elopment interventions that we associate above all with the work of Albert Hirschman: can the errors inevitably committed by large-scale development projects and organizations be mitigated by in-built 'self-correcting mechanisms'? Starting from ideas in Hirschman's *Development Projects Observed* (1967), Arturo Israel has expanded the concept of 'specificity', which refers to self-correcting mechanisms intrinsic to the nature of the functions that organizations perform. We pursue here a different strand of Hirschman's work: potential self-correcting mechan-isms rooted in the responses of clients to programme failures. The best point of departure is *Exit, Voice and Loyalty* (1970) in which Hirschman explores the conditions under which dissatisfied clients will pursue exit or voice strategies in relation to the organization. Samuel Paul (1992) has extended these ideas by exploring, in a deductive fashion, the ways in which particular services – e.g. rural health facilities, urban transport or university education – might stimulate exit or voice by virtue of the intrinsic character of the services themselves. For example, urban low-income housing is expected to generate high exit and low voice; and electricity to encourage high voice and low exit. Paul's work has not had much impact. We believe this is because he has focused too narrowly on the potential *technical* implications of different services, and abstracted from the *sociological and political* concerns that are central to this chapter. Our contribution is therefore to redirect attention to the ways in which the relationships between poor people and external agencies affect the responses of the poor to programmes initiated from outside.

Our second source of theoretical inspiration lies in the question of what – in the relative calm following the dethroning of neo-liberal doctrine – we believe we have learned from it. Implicit in the paper is firm support for a normative position that unites most prominent critics of neo-liberalism, notably the theorists of institutionalism, social capital, trust and participation: an appreciation that strong social networks are often crucial to the effective functioning of political, bureaucratic and market systems, and that the utilitarianism that lies behind neo-liberalism continues, as ever, to provide us with analytical models of society that are partial and misleading and with public policy prescriptions that are often arid and impractical.[1] On the other side, we share with neo-liberalism (i) a focus on the 'leakage' problem in public distribution programmes and (ii) a preference for governance arrangements that involve creating an 'enabling environment' for societal agents rather than more direct and directive state interventions. But the implications of this latter point for anti-poverty interventions need to be made much more explicit. Due largely to the influence of neo-liberalism, it is now a development policy orthodoxy that governments should strive to create 'enabling environments' for private investors. Our argument is that the same should be done for the poor. Let them also enjoy the 'level playing field' that business these days so often demands of governments. For the poor, enabling environments and level playing fields will take the form of public anti-poverty interventions disciplined by the concerns about *predictability* explored here, to increase the chances that the poor will be able to mobilize on their own terms and take advantage of the public resources formally directed at them.

THE CENTRALITY OF THE IMPLEMENTATION STAGE

There is no scarcity of 'design level' ideas about effective anti-poverty interventions. There is a rich literature on, for example: targeting (Van Der Walle 1998); appropriate wage levels for public works; and making micro-credit accessible to the poor (Hulme and Mosley 1996). Yet programme outcomes are often disappointing. We need to look more at what works in practice. The outcomes of public programmes to tackle poverty are especially likely, in poor countries, to be decided in the 'implementation' rather than the 'decision' phases of policy-making.[2] There are three separate reasons for this.

First, in poor countries, the implementation stage tends to be particularly significant in all spheres and sectors of public action, not simply anti-poverty interventions. It is plausibly argued that this is the defining feature of 'third world politics': because of the generally low level of political institutionalization, discretionary decisions made by bureaucrats and politicians at the implementation stage shape actual allocations of public resources to a greater extent than in the advanced countries, where government processes are more open, procedures more formal and predictable, and encompassing interest groups better organized to hold governments to account (Grindle and Thomas 1991: ch. 3; Horowitz 1989).

Second, in so far as jobs, houses, food rations, transport subsidies, school places and medical services formally intended for the poor are actually appropriated by the non-poor (the neo-liberal prediction), it is in the implementation stage that this is especially likely to occur. Poor people generally lack political resources. This is particularly true in poor countries, where they are likely to be physically dispersed and face high transport and communication costs; to be ill-educated; to be (partially) excluded from the public sphere because they cannot understand the language or dialect of elites and government; and to face government agencies and bureaucratic processes that are weakly institutionalized, informal and accessible mainly to those who have privileged personal or social connections. Those connections can most effectively be employed during implementation.

Third, and especially in poor countries characterized by high degrees of income inequality and socio-political polarization, reformist regimes and politicians often use the implementation phase to redistribute income or assets to the poor in non-transparent ways, trying to avoid mobilizing the opposition of the wealthy and powerful by providing them with few specific targets or grievances (Ascher 1984).

THE CONCEPTUAL FRAMEWORK

If the poor are especially likely to lose out during the implementation of anti-poverty interventions, it follows that it is important to try to plug the gaps at this stage. There are many potential mechanisms for doing this. In this chapter we focus on an important but neglected issue: the ways in which anti-poverty interventions might be designed to be 'self-correcting', in the sense that they encourage actual and potential poor beneficiaries to 'mobilize' to advance their interests. 'Mobilization' refers to collective action. Collective action, however, takes many forms. In the context of relationships between the poor and public agencies, there is a continuum. At one end, the poor are completely subordinated, they are mobilized to engage in collective action by public agencies in terms set by public agencies.[3] The prevalent popularity of 'participation' in programmes has, in practice, mostly tended to stay at this end. Often, even in the most participatory programmes, there is little interest in whether poor people are engaged in collective action to make demands on the state, to enforce their rights or to engage in political action for change. At the other end of the continuum, the poor are in open conflict with public agencies.[4] We deal here with intermediate ranges on this continuum, where one can reasonably think of 'reform-mongering' that might be in the interests of the poor.

Many factors, especially the overall character of national politics, influence the scope for any kind of mobilization around anti-poverty interventions. We focus here on the question of how, all other factors being equal, anti-poverty programmes can be designed either (i) positively to encourage the mobilization of poor beneficiaries or (ii) less ambitious, so that they do not actively discourage it. We know that the *content* of anti-poverty interventions – the resources that the potential beneficiaries stand to gain – can affect their willingness to engage in collective action.[5] We are concerned here not with programme content in the narrow sense, but with the *relationship* between the poor and public agencies that is implicit in the design and management of anti-poverty interventions. In what circumstances can that relationship encourage the mobilization that will in turn enable the poor to obtain greater benefits from those interventions?

One could try to answer that question empirically, examining the specific circumstances of a wide variety of cases. This chapter focuses on a prior stage: developing the conceptual and theoretical tools needed to undertake such an exercise. Our overarching concept is *predictability*: the predictability or various dimensions of anti-poverty interventions from the perspective of poor people and of the social activists and political entrepreneurs who are needed to stimulate and lead them into collective action.[6] Drawing from examples of anti-poverty programmes we suggest three sub-categories of the concept of predictability, each of them referring to a different dimension of the relationship between public agencies and the poor in the context of anti-poverty interventions:

- *Credibility.* This refers to the *behaviour* of public officials in relation to the poor: the extent to which officials implementing anti-poverty interventions can be relied on to behave like good partners in an

enterprise, i.e. to do their job correctly and to behave predictably.
- *Programme stability*. This refers to the extent to which anti-poverty programmes are *stable over time in content, form, procedural requirements* and so on.
- *Formal entitlement*. This relates to the *legal and normative status of benefits* from anti-poverty programmes: the extent to which intended beneficiaries are entitled to appeal to alternative, formal channels if anti-poverty programmes fail to deliver appropriate services. Like the other sub-categories above, this is a continuous and somewhat diffuse concept. Recourse to personal connections with politicians may result in effective but not very formal entitlement. The most formal type of entitlement is a legal right – that may or may not be very accessible to poor people in practice.

Credibility, programme stability and formal entitlement are means not ends. And the extent to which they are useful means towards the end (more effective anti-poverty programmes) depends on context. More does not always mean better. For example, low levels of credibility on the part of public officials may *sometimes* serve to stimulate useful collective action on the part of those adversely affected.[7] Such cases are not typical. High levels of predictability *generally* help induce the collective action needed to make anti-poverty interventions work better. Different types of predictability are, however, required to encourage and support different types of collective action. We illustrate that argument with two case studies.

Credibility and concordant collective action   Our first example comes from a rural drinking water supply programme in Nepal that was funded by the Finnish aid agency, FINNIDA, and implemented by a Finnish consultancy company with expatriate and local staff.[8] The programme design was relatively orthodox. Water projects in the mountains of Nepal are expensive; most costs were met by FINNIDA. Communities that chose to participate were required to organize themselves to make inputs into planning, construction, fee collection and maintenance. Although they contributed only a fraction of construction costs, their total commitments, in terms of cash, labour and self-organization, were significant to them; this was not an exercise that a community would embark on lightly. Nepali government agencies undertook the investigation, design work and much of the construction, under the eye of the aid project staff. The programme had been in operation for six years – long enough for us to judge it a success in terms of both process and outcome. A large number of water supply schemes had been built without glaring design or construction failures. As far as we could judge, villagers had made a substantial input in most cases and exhibited a degree of ownership.

We asked villagers why and how they became involved in this programme. The lessons we learned are encapsulated from the responses in two different villages:

Village A: 'We had wanted water for a long time. We heard that the Fanta Company had done a good job in Villages V and W, so we talked to them about their experience and then approached the Company.' (In many places, FINNIDA had been transmuted into 'Fanta Company'. Fanta is a popular soft drink in South Asia.)

Village B: We asked why it had taken the villagers three years from the time the water project was first mooted until they began to make serious progress to get themselves organized and raise resources: 'We have had at least four different survey teams here from the Local Government Department over the past fifteen years, promising us water. They come when there is an election. We don't really trust people who come and talk about bringing us water. It took us a long time to learn to trust these people. We discovered that they had done good work elsewhere and seemed reliable.'

The 'reliability' of which the villagers talked is what we have termed *credibility*. It refers to both technical competence and dependability when interacting with others. Water projects are expensive and vulnerable to poor location (especially via landslips), poor design and bad construction. If Nepali villagers invest their efforts and savings in a water project that fails or is simply never completed, they lose a great deal. The perceived reliability of the external agent is central to the willingness of communities to mobilize their own contributions. These conversations heightened our awareness that much of the interaction between poor people and external agencies is shaped by rational lack of trust on the part of poor people. Increasingly, they are bombarded by visitors from outside who ask for something from them (even if only their time in meetings) and often promise or imply some reward for co-operation. 'Someone will be back'; 'You will hear more'; 'Ask the Council Chairman in a couple of months'. To us, these outsiders fall into distinct categories: politicians; researchers; government officials; students; census officials; World Bank visitors; aid agency staff on familiarization tours;

Christian missionaries; NGO staffers; consultants. It is much more difficult for villagers to draw such distinctions, to get any accurate sense of what the agenda actually is, or, above all, to get any kind of binding commitment from outsiders in return for co-operating with them. By contrast, external agencies that have established a reputation for *credibility* on the basis of their performance are at least serious candidates for trust.

People who know the rural water sector in Nepal might be tempted to read our case as an illustration of the badness of the government sector and the virtues of NGOs. For, while formally in the public sector, the 'Fanta Company' in practice enjoyed the operational and budgetary autonomy of an NGO. There is, however, a clear and important contrast between the strategies employed by the 'Fanta Company' on the one hand and most NGOs on the other to tackle the problem of villagers' rational suspicion of outsiders promising water. The staff of Nepali NGOs working in the sector presented us with an image of their relative strengths that could have been obtained in almost any developing country. Government agencies were inefficient and corrupt; they took a very long time to get anything done; did it at high cost; and then delivered only standard designs in standard ways, completely disregarding the specific needs, preferences and capacities of different groups of clients. By contrast, we were told that NGOs could find out what people wanted, work with local communities, ensure that appropriate low-cost designs were used, and generally get a good job done cheaply. There was in Nepal at that time friction between NGOs and government water agencies, fuelled by competition for aid funds. This was articulated in terms of relative professional competence. The government water agencies were equally critical of the NGOs, claiming that the NGOs were working with shoddy designs that of course could be constructed cheaply and quickly, but soon fell apart; and that they were experimenting so much, without consistency or good records, that the government agencies were left with an almighty mess when they were asked to maintain and rehabilitate the water facilities that the NGOs had constructed in ones and two all over the country.

It was no surprise to us that spokesmen of government agencies made little reference to what we have termed *credibility* issues. That the NGOs were aware of them is implicit in the procedure they typically adopted: sending social mobilizers into villages for weeks or months to gain the trust and co-operation of the population before initiating construction work. We doubt that this 'active marketing' strategy – taking the initiative to persuade villagers to co-operate through establishing new and positive social relations with them – is the best solution to the distrust problem. The 'passive marketing' strategy employed by the 'Fanta Company' – i.e. set some good examples of *credibility* and then rely on reputation to interest other villagers and elicit requests for assistance – appears superior. It implies a high and often justified faith in the capacity of communities to organize themselves once they are confident that they have reliable external partners. This obviates the need for external social mobilizers, and provides a more valid test of community engagement and sense of ownership than do commitments made in response to 'active marketing' strategies employed by influential outsiders. We have to assume that social mobilizers generally are biased in favour of obtaining formal commitments from communities to engage in projects. This will enhance both their careers and their sense of job satisfaction. The organizations that employ them are also vulnerable to the moral hazard of temptation to abuse the 'active marketing' route. What is to stop an effective social mobilizer from persuading villagers to co-operate on schemes that are badly designed or constructed but look good on the papers that go to the aid donors? The social mobilizer is anyway leaving the village once the project is complete, and the relative inaccessibility of most of rural Nepal means that few aid projects are ever independently and properly assessed. Could it be true, as alleged to us, that NGOs sometimes 'saved' vast sums of money and cut short construction times by, for example, hanging polythene water pipes between trees rather than burying them deep in the ground out of harm's way? Perhaps the impressive performances that some of them were reporting really were based on misuse, unintended or conscious, of a position of power that they had established through their marketing techniques? Note that there was a clear affinity between this 'active marketing' strategy and the fact that many NGOs were working on a very small scale, often spreading their resources widely over more than one locality – a village here and a village there. The more charitable interpretation of the consequences of this wide scattering of activities is that it provided little scope for building up local reputations for *credibility*. The more sceptical view is that it protected NGOs against performance scrutiny and helped maintain their dominance in their relationships with the communities where they were working.

The water projects we have discussed here work better if local people engage in collective action and invest substantial resources in collaboration with external agencies, all the time ensuring that the collaboration takes place on equal terms. If they are to make substantial investments in planning and construction, communities need a *concordant* relationship – both generalized trust and extensive co-operation in implementation. The *credibility* of the external agency, and the reputation it thereby acquired, were central to project success. *Programme stability* was a secondary factor, of some significance. Communities needed some assurance that their external partner would be around long enough to ensure completion of individual projects. Although the programme that we studied was aid funded and very likely to come to an end within a few years, it had been operating for six years and worked through the permanent Nepali government agencies. *Entitlement* played no significant role. There was no legal recourse for villagers if things went wrong, and very little political recourse: the programme was relatively insulated from Nepali politics, and project mistakes and failures are easily concealed from external evaluators in the Nepali hills and mountains.

Programme stability, formal entitlement and discordant collective action Our second example deals with a different type of anti-poverty intervention; a relationship between the poor and external agencies that was frequently *discordant*; and the ways in which *programme stability* and *formal entitlement* helped sustain a more overtly politicized kind of popular mobilization.

In the mid-1970s, the state of Maharashtra, India, introduced an Employment Guarantee Scheme (EGS) for its rural population – assured unskilled employment on local public works on request. The EGS appeared innovative and received attention in its early years. Over the twenty-three years from 1975/6 to 1998/9, it has provided an annual average of 132 million work days, on 341,661 separate work sites – soil and water conservation, small-scale irrigation, reforestation and local roads. Despite many problems, EGS continues to provide relatively cost-effective and reliable social security for significant sections of the rural poor of Maharashtra. We have recently been conducting field and documentary research on EGS, focusing on the 'guarantee' and the role of client mobilization in making the scheme work.[9] Our conclusions are encouraging.

EGS is an innovative scheme for providing paid work for the rural poor on a self-selection basis, with (i) a substantial in-built guarantee of work and (ii) a set of procedures for using this labour to construct public infrastructure. The precise procedures and conditions offered under EGS to achieve these goals have changed over the years. It is convenient here to summarize the situation when the scheme was formalized in the mid-1970s. All rural adults over the age of eighteen who were willing to do manual unskilled work on a piece-rate basis were offered a guarantee of employment within fifteen days of the demand being made, provided that (i) jobseekers registered with the local administration; and (ii) there were at least fifty jobseekers in one locality. In principle – although almost never in practice – the government was obliged to pay an un-employment benefit (originally Rs 1 per day) if it was unable to provide suitable work for registered jobseekers. More significant, if the job offered was more than 5 km from the residence of the jobseeker, the government was obliged to provide a specified set of amenities, including temporary housing and childcare facilities. Although there is no single comprehensive set of figures, most sources indicate that around half of all EGS employment has gone to women. On the government side, EGS committees identified and designed shelves of projects, so that the scheme could be operationalized at short notice during the dry, lean season and during unusual droughts. Projects were required to create productive assets. At least 60 per cent of expenditures were to be on unskilled labour. Soil and water conservation drought prevention works were given priority. EGS operates through two parallel lines of adminis-tration: the Revenue Department (i.e. territorial administration) that controls the financing, opening and closing of projects and directs workers to appropriate sites; and various technical departments (Irriga-tion, Agriculture, Forestry, Highways) that identify and design particular projects and manage the construction process.

What makes EGS distinctive is the fact that it is enshrined in state law. The implementation details – wage rates, eligibility conditions, criteria for projects – can be, and are, changed by the executive authority of the state government. But the Maharashtra Employment Guarantee Act of 1977 obliges the government of Maharashtra to operate an Employment Guarantee Scheme for the rural poor. Equally important, the Maharashtra State Tax on Professions, Trades, Callings and Employ-ments Act of 1975 provides a dedicated financing mechanism, i.e. a revenue stream devoted to EGS. There are five specific taxes, of which the most important is the 'professional tax' that is borne mainly by registered professionals and formal sector employees in the urban areas.

The state government is obliged to make a contribution to the Employment Guarantee Fund that matches the yield from these dedicated taxes. Once the Secretary to the government of Maharashtra (EGS) has certified in an appropriate fashion that funds are required to honour the employment guarantee, the state government is legally obliged to release the money.

How did such progressive ideas ever get on to the statute books? Without going into details we might mention that a large component of it is responses to a major drought that affected large areas of Western Maharashtra in 1970–74. The massive public works programme mounted to deal with the consequences of drought provided the basis on which EGS became a state-wide programme. The state government responded effectively to the drought, in part because the communist and left political parties and trades unions rooted in Mumbai (Bombay), the state capital, had established bases in the drought areas. They organized many 'agitations' and sparked a fear of more general unrest.[10]

The more important question for us is why EGS has continued to be implemented relatively effectively, in a country where there often appear to be several public programmes for every conceivable development problem, most of them quickly mired in clientelist politics and/or corruption. There are partial answers to that question that we are unable to explore in detail here. They include the fact that there is a balance of power between two distinct sections of the state apparatus: the 'line departments' that implement EGS projects (Irrigation, Agriculture, Forestry, Highways); and the Revenue Department (general territorial administration) that controls the finances and constitutes the channel through which demands for work are expressed and, more generally, political concerns and pressures are treated. It is also important that, in response to revelations of corruption, the mechanisms for checking and approving EGS expenditures are demanding and relatively transparent. However, these particular parts of the explanation function mainly because EGS jobseekers, or their political representatives, are mobilized to demand their rights. And that in turn can be attributed mainly to two features of the scheme.

One is that the general principles on which EGS is constructed provide opportunities for intermediary organizations and politicians to create a role and make a name for themselves. At the operational level, EGS work is temporary, seasonal and dependent in part on the weather; there is no permanent labour force and little natural solidarity around a common long-term place of work. Minimum numbers of people need to be brought together and government officers approached to trigger the job-providing mechanism. Someone needs to do that. And there are rights, legally or administratively mandated, that can be asserted: rights to a job within a given time period; specific employment conditions, such as the provision of adequate temporary housing or water; daily work norms required for the piece-rate wages; the adjustment of these wages for inflation. There have been *morchas* (marches) *dharnas* (sit-ins) and *gheraos* (sieges of government offices) at many levels. EGS is not the labour organizers' dream. Above all, it provides no scope for the use of the strike weapon: if eligible jobseekers strike, the government simply saves money. Nevertheless, EGS provides wide opportunities for grassroots activists and politicians to cut their teeth and show their worth by (i) seizing the opportunities for intermediation created by the operational procedures and (ii) asserting rights. Trades unions and other activist organizations have played a role here, but it is local politicians who dominate. These intermediaries are often much better informed than poor people about the rights embodied in EGS. The interests of the poor and the intermediaries, however, largely coincide, and this is what keeps the 'guarantee' element of the scheme alive.

The fact that EGS is entrenched in law also creates opportunities for political intermediation through the courts. In 1989, a coalition of left and trades union activists based in the city of Ahmednagar, a prime district for EGS employment, won a moral victory in the Mumbai High Court, when the government of Maharashtra was ordered to review the fact that the unemployment allowance – paid to registered EGS job-seekers who could not be given employment – was both paltry in size and almost never paid in practice. In 1999, a coalition of Mumbai-based activists went to court because the government of Maharashtra had increased the Professional Tax used to finance EGS despite the fact that the EGS Fund was increasingly underspent. The intention was to try to force the state government to pay more attention to using unspent EGS funds to tackle continuing problems of rural unemployment. The Mumbai High Court declared that it had no jurisdiction over the case. It is currently on appeal to the Supreme Court.

The second reason why there is so much constructive political mobilization around EGS rights is that the scheme has been in place for twenty years, is well institutionalized and operates throughout the state. Knowledge of how to 'work' the scheme accumulates over time; and it is worthwhile for politicians and social activists to invest in developing this knowledge because they have a high degree of confidence that EGS will be in place next year and the year after. Unlike other government programmes, it is not easy for newly elected state governments to abolish EGS and replace it with another anti-poverty programme, precisely because it is legislated. The contribution of these two factors – the existence of intermediation opportunities based on rights (formal entitlement) and a permanent, uniform presence (programme stability) – to the mobilization that has helped guarantee the effectiveness of EGS can better be demonstrated by comparing it briefly with similar public employment programmes.

Impressed by the reputation of EGS, and no doubt wishing not to appear less effective or concerned than a state government in dealing with rural unemployment, the (federal) government of India has introduced national public works employment programmes that it funds directly. The Employment Assurance Scheme (EAS), introduced in 1994, in one respect *appears* better targeted than EGS because preference should be given to members of households below the poverty line. EAS was often described to us as 'identical to EGS – except for the lack of a guarantee of work'. That is the administrators' perspective. For the 'except for the guarantee' is crucial. There is no mobilization around EAS, because the lever of rights is lacking. It is the *entitlement* to employment that limits bureaucratic discretion and ensures that, to a substantial degree, EGS opportunities really are targeted on the poor.

Activists trying to mobilize the poor around anti-poverty interventions require programmes that are rights-based and sufficiently stable over time and consistent over space that it is worth investing time and energy in acquiring relevant knowledge and building appropriate networks and institutions. From the perspective of grassroots activism, *programme stability* and *formal entitlement* are valuable assets. The fact that they have often involved *discordant* relationships with the local state apparatus has contributed to rather than detracted from their effectiveness. However, this discordance has not been popular with the state apparatus. Local administrators have used the discretion they enjoy to try to suppress local activism. They have had some success, but are still constrained by the strong rights element built into EGS, the relative autonomy and power of the Indian courts, and the institutionalization of mobilization around the right to work. The creators of the EGS merit an award for clever political and institutional design.

PREDICTABILITY AND CONTEMPORARY POLICY

There are good reasons to believe that (i) credibility, programme stability and formal entitlement often contribute to programme effectiveness through encouraging 'watchdog' activities and (ii) that their potential contribution is widely ignored. Indeed, it would be surprising if this were not both ignored and downplayed. For the main sponsors and deliverers of anti-poverty interventions, whether government agencies or NGOs, face less criticism and have an easier life if their clients are unorganized or organized purely on the agencies' own terms.

How relevant are these predictability concerns to the shape of contemporary anti-poverty interventions in poor countries? There is a great deal of national variation and that makes generalizations risky. There are, however, two widespread policy trends that give grounds for concern. Although contemporary anti-poverty policies tend formally to be justified in terms of concepts such as 'participation' and responsiveness to client needs, there appears in practice to be little concern for the issues and relationships we have discussed here.

First, there has been a big expansion in the use of NGOs as agents for the delivery of public services to the poor. We can look again at Maharashtra to illustrate the consequences. Maharashtra is a relatively developed and politically aware state in the Indian context. It enjoys a history of extensive popular and leftist political activity, and, since the 1980s, has shared in the big expansion of the activities of development NGOs. Some rural activists blamed the slackening of political activity around the Employment Guarantee Scheme and related issues in the late 1980s and early 1990s on the growth of (foreign-funded) NGOs. These NGOs are said to be attractive to employers, and to have 'seduced' the rural activists who had previously helped mobilize the poor around issues of a broadly 'class' nature. Whatever the degree of truth in that charge, it is clear that the development activities of NGOs do not elicit the same kind of countervailing popular organization that the EGS has generated. NGOs provide pure 'benefits', not entitlements in either the moral or legal sense of the term. There is no moral or legal basis on which to organize to ensure that NGOs deliver what they promise. Equally important, NGO activities are invariably small scale and dispersed, and frequently experimental and in practice flexible, temporary and unstable. To the NGO staffers and their funders, flexibility and experimentation are positive values that contribute to 'learning experiences'. To potential social activists these same values are disabling, for NGO implementation undermines the scope for mobilization of the poor around programme implementation. We will not dwell too much on the impact of the induction of grassroots activists into an NGO and programme implementation 'establishment'. This is certainly a widespread phenomenon (e.g. Clarke 1998: 208). More important are the points made above that (i) NGO programmes typically are diverse, fragmented and unstable (they lack programme stability); and (ii) they are not even potentially formally enforceable in the way that programmes run directly by government agencies may be. The wider use of NGOs for service delivery is sometimes defended or justified on the grounds that NGOs are better able to mobilize the poor. Some element of mobilization is often built into programmes implemented by NGOs. To that degree, there is a potential counter-argument to the one we have advanced. We are, however, sceptical of the capacity or willingness of any but the most exceptional organizations to encourage or even tolerate the autonomous and potentially antagonistic mobilization of their client groups.

Second, and despite the rhetorical and substantive shift to the NGO sector, there has been a massive expansion of one particular type of public anti-poverty programme: the so-called 'Social Funds'.[11] The amounts of money involved are enormous. Social Funds are thick on the ground in Latin America, and fairly common in Africa. They were originally justified mainly in terms of coping with the social costs of economic adjustment. They have become the dominant anti-poverty instrument of the international financial institutions and banks, and are spreading to Asia. The main aid donors committed substantial money to deal with the social costs of the recent implosion of the Indonesian economy only when a Social Fund was put in place in late 1998. It is estimated that, since the late 1980s, the World Bank, the Inter-American Development Bank and the main European aid donors spent about US$4 billion on Social Funds in Latin America and Africa (Tendler 1999: 1).

Although Social Funds come in many shapes and sizes, a core component, both substantively and ideologically, is the idea of response to 'community demand'. Most Social Fund expenditure is committed by asking poor territorially-defined 'communities' to decide how they would like to spend an external cash injection for community purposes. Do they want a water supply system or a tool-shed? A road or a new school building? A tractor or latrines? Social Funds are managed by a special bureaucratic agency, and private firms and NGOs are frequently commissioned to undertake preparation, design and construction work. The rhetoric is of decentralization; moving away from the monolithic state and its 'old-fashioned', unresponsive specialist departments (water, irrigation, health, agriculture etc.); tapping the strengths of the private sector and NGOs; and, above all, shifting from 'supply-driven' to 'demand-driven' service delivery. From our particular perspective on anti-poverty programmes then, Social Funds are expected to encourage the mobilization of beneficiaries.

The reality is not only more complex but substantially different. To a large degree, the real choices are made somewhere up the line by politicians, by bureaucrats, or by the private companies and NGOs who are formally supposed to elicit community desires. There are a number of interacting reasons for this situation, but the dominant factor is that the implementation of Social Funds is weak in all three dimensions of predictability that we have identified: credibility, programme stability and formal entitlement. Communities are presented with their Social Funds opportunity out of the blue. They face what appears to be a once in a lifetime opportunity, since the programmes are not so well funded or established that they become a regular part of the annual round in any community. Information on the resources actually available is limited. Publicity campaigns are poor – not because governments do not know how to run such campaigns, but because every agency in a position of authority has a strong interest in limiting information, so that they can influence community choice. Politicians do not want accurate and transparent information, since that would (i) reduce their discretion to grant access for political reasons and (ii) lead to excess demands for access to Social Funds that would generate political disappointment. Government agencies do not want to generate more demand than they can handle, and generally find some types of community projects easier to handle than others. They want both to limit demands and standardize the types of facilities they supply. And the private companies that design and construct projects also want to standardize, because that reduces costs and increases profits. Since these are all 'one-shot games' as far as any individual community is concerned, there is little opportunity to build up knowledge of what is really on offer, and how best to bargain with these better informed external agencies.

The Social Funds case is very similar to that of the NGOs: a new set of institutional arrangements for delivering public services to the poor are justified through the rhetoric to 'community', 'client demand', 'localism' and 'decentralization', while little real attention is paid to creating an organizational context that will help the poor actually to organize to ensure that programmes work in their favour. Both cases illustrate the main point of our argument: mobilizing the poor effectively might better be done by paying less attention to sending emissaries, organizers and propagandists down to the grassroots, and putting more effort into providing the poor with an enabling external bureaucratic and programme environment – one characterized by more predictability than one is used to encountering.

NOTES

We are grateful to many people in Nepal and Maharashtra, India, for permitting and helping us do the field research on which this chapter is based; to the participants of the workshop on 'Best Practices in Poverty Research', Jordan, 10 November 1999, for useful comments and suggestions; and to the UK Department for International Development (DFID) for support to the IDS Poverty Research Programme within which the ideas here were developed.

1. It is not possible here to provide more than a few sample references to these alternatives to neo-liberalism: on social capital, Putnam (1993) and Woolcock (1998); on trust, Gambetta and Fukuyama (1995); and on institutionalism, Immergut (1998) and March and Olsen (1996).

2. The distinction between 'implementation' and 'decision' is highly problematic, but we have no alternative language in which to discuss these issues.

3. It was to this that Selznik was referring when he described participation as 'a technique for turning an unorganised citizenry into a reliable instrument for the achievement of administrative goals' (Selznik 1949: 84). These issues are generally treated under the term 'corporatism' (Cawson 1986).

4. The radical view is that this is the only way of ensuring that the voice of the poor is heard (e.g. Piven and Cloward 1971).

5. For example, it appears generally true that poor people are motivated above all by the prospect of relatively immediate and tangible resources (Salamon and Lund 1989: 44).

6. Most theoretical work on collective action follows the lead set by Mancur Olson (1965), focuses on the incentives for individual agents to participate, and underplays the significance of leadership roles and strategies. While adhering to the Olsonian rational choice framework, Dunleavy (1991: ch. 3) has reformulated the theory of group action to allow for the importance of leadership.

7. The general point is that conflict between groups often stimulates solidarity within them (Coser 1956).

8. We undertook some research on this programme in 1996. See Moore and al. (1996).

9. There is a large literature on EGS, most of it published in India. The more internationally accessible sources are: Acharya (1990); Dev (1996); Echeverri-Gent (1993); Gaiha (1996 and 1997); and Herring and Edwards (1983).

10. Another part of the story is found in changes in state boundaries and in the fact that in the late 1960s power within the ruling Maharashtra Congress Party shifted decisively from Mumbai-based industrial and commercial capitalists, most of them non-Marathi speakers and thus 'outsiders' to the new linguistic-based state of Maharashtra. The people who inherited power were mainly big farmers and rural commercial interests of the Maratha caste, many based in the drought affected areas of Western Maharashtra. EGS was essentially funded by a tax on Mumbai. It was in part an expression of the political dominance of this new Marathi-speaking, rural-based class.

11. This section is based heavily on Judith Tendler's recent thorough review of the Social Funds (Tendler 1999). For more corroborating analyses from the agencies financing Social Funds, see for example, Inter-American Development Bank (1998).

REFERENCES

Acharya, S. (1990) 'The Maharashtra Employment Guarantee Scheme: A Study of Labour Market Intervention', *ARTEP Working Paper* (Delhi: International Labour Organization/Asian Regional Team for Employment Promotion).

Ascher, W. (1984) *Scheming for the Poor. The Politics of Redistribution in Latin America* (Cambridge, MA and London: Harvard University Press).

Cawson, A. (1986) *Corporatism and Political Theory* (Oxford: Basil Blackwell).

Clarke, G. (1998) *The Politics of NGOs in South-East Asia. Participation and Protest in the Philippines* (London: Routledge).

Coser, L. A. (1956) *The Functions of Social Conflict* (London: Routledge).

Dev, M. (1996) 'Experience of India's (Maharashtra) Employment Guarantee Scheme: Lessons for Development Policy', *Development Policy Review*, Vol. 14, no. 3, pp. 227–53.

Dunleavy, P. (1991) *Democracy, Bureaucracy and Public Choice. Economic Explanations in Political Science* (New York and London: Harvester/Wheatsheaf).

Echeverri-Gent, J. (1993) *The State and the Poor. Public Policy and Political Development in India and the United States* (Berkeley, CA: University of California Press).

Fukuyama, F. (1995) *Trust: The Social Virtues and the Creation of Prosperity* (London: Hamish Hamilton).

Gaiha, R. (1996) 'How Dependent are the Rural Poor on the Employment Guarantee Scheme in India?', *Journal of Development Studies*, Vol. 32, no. 5, pp. 669–94.

— (1997) 'Do Rural Public Works Influence Agricultural Wages? The Case of the Employment Guarantee Scheme in India', *Oxford Development Studies*, Vol. 25, no. 3, pp. 301–14.

Gambetta, D. (ed.) (1988) *Trust. The Making and Breaking of Cooperative Relations* (Oxford: Basil Blackwell).

Grindle, M. S. and J. W. Thomas (1991) *Public Choice and Policy Change. The Political Economy of Reform in Developing Countries* (Baltimore and London: Johns Hopkins University Press).

Herring, R. and R. M. Edwards (1983) 'Guaranteeing Employment to the Rural

Poor: Social Functions and Class Interests in the Employment Guarantee Scheme in Western India', *World Development*, Vol. 11, No. 7, pp. 575–92.

Hirschman, A. O. (1967) *Development Projects Observed* (Washington, DC: Brookings Institution).

— (1970) *Exit, Voice, and Loyalty* (Cambridge, MA: Harvard University Press).

Horowitz, D. L. (1989) 'Is There a Third World Policy Process?', *Policy Sciences*, Vol 22, pp. 197–212.

Hulme, D. and P. Mosley (1996) *Finance Against Poverty* (London: Routledge).

Immergut, E. M. (1998) 'The Theoretical Core of the New Institutionalism', *Politics and Society*, Vol. 26, no. 1, pp. 5–34.

Inter-American Development Bank (1998) 'The Use of Social Funds as an Instrument for Combating Poverty', *IDB Sector Strategy*, POV-104 (Washington, DC: Inter-American Development Bank).

Israel, A. (1987) *Institutional Development. Incentives to Performance* (Baltimore: Johns Hopkins University Press).

March, J. G. and J. P. Olsen (1996) 'Institutional Perspectives on Political Institutions', *Governance*, Vol. 9, no. 3, pp. 247–64.

Moore, M. et. al. (1996) 'Ownership in the Finnish Aid Programme', *Evaluation Study*, 1996: 3, Ministry of Foreign Affairs of Finland, Department for International Development Cooperation.

Olson, M. (1965) *The Logic of Collective Action* (Cambridge, MA: Harvard University Press).

Paul, S. (1992) 'Accountability in Public Services: Exit, Voice and Control', *World Development*, Vol. 20, no. 7, pp. 1047–61.

Piven, F. F. and R. A. Cloward (1971) *Regulating the Poor. The Functions of Public Welfare* (New York: Vintage Books).

Putnam, R. (1993) *Making Democracy Work. Civic Traditions in Modern Italy* (Princeton, NJ: Princeton University Press).

Salamon, L. M. and M. S. Lund (1989) 'The Tools Approach: Basic Analytics', in L. M. Salamon (ed.), *Beyond Privatization: The Tools of Government Action* (Washington, DC: Urban Institute Press).

Selznick, P. (1949) *T.V.A. and the Grassroots: A Study in the Sociology of Formal Organizations* (Berkeley, CA: California University Press).

Stiglitz, J. E. (1998) 'More Instruments and Broader Goals: Moving Beyond the Post-Washington Consensus', *Wider Annual Lectures*, 2 (Helsinki: WIDER).

Tendler, J. (1999) 'The Rise of Social Funds: What are They a Model of?', *Draft Report for MIT/UNDP Decentralisation Project* (Cambridge, MA: Massachusetts Institute of Technology).

Van Der Walle, D. (1998) 'Targeting Revisited', *World Bank Research Observer*, Vol. 13, no. 2, pp. 231–48.

Woolcock, M. (1998) 'Social Capital and Economic Development: Toward a Theoretical Synthesis and Policy Framework', *Theory and Society*, Vol. 27, no. 2, pp. 151–208.

World Bank (1997) *World Development Report 1997: The State in a Changing World* (New York: Oxford University Press).

THREE

Best Practices: Scepticism and Hope

S. M. MILLER

WHY 'BEST PRACTICES'?

What is very encouraging about the language of 'best practices' is that it encourages large-scale programmes. The contrasting policy approach promotes small-scale 'model' programmes that seldom become the template for major programmes. Many nations attempt 'demonstration projects' that never grow beyond this beginning stage of policy development.[1] Even worse is the adoption of untested programmes because they appear attractive. The discourse of 'best practices' implies evaluations that lead to large-scale programmes to aid the many.[2]

The adjective 'best' connotes a level of policy achievement and scientific certainty that is hard to attain. Consequently, less demanding standards are offered. One such alternative to 'best practices' is 'promising practices', used in a presidential report on race in the United States.[3] A more comprehensive but differently oriented approach than these perspectives is that of 'poverty proofing', requiring exploration of the effects on the poor of all governmental policies, not only those directed at reducing poverty.[4]

The lure of 'best practices' runs the danger of offering a 'scientism', overstating the level of accomplishment of social science and seeking to have social scientists use their data interpretations to make what are at some level political decisions. Relying on presumably scientific procedures to determine policy is likely to be misleading and possibly dangerous; misleading because it assumes that social scientific work delivers definitive answers rather than probabilities.[5] Furthermore, the on-the-ground conditions for valid comparative evaluations are hard to achieve. Dangerous because it provides a 'scientific' cover for decisions for which politicians should be responsible and removes decisions away from the political arena where the choices should be made.

THE QUESTIONS

Determining what constitutes a 'best practice' is not straightforward and many questions have to be addressed.[6]

The assumption in much of the discourse about best practice is that a practice or programme has a clear, single purpose. Many evaluators are surprised and dismayed by the discovery that programmes often have diffuse, multiple objectives. For example, increasing productivity in low-income agricultural areas may be the main goal but it may also be linked to a plan to encourage some smaller farmers to leave an unfertile area. The two objectives may not be equally important but they are significant when comparing two approaches to improving productivity.

A goal is frequently, if not usually, attached to an 'and' that specifies a second or third objective. The additional goals might be considered constraints on the main objective and they impede the definitive specification of a goal that is to be achieved.

The assumption made in many careful evaluations is that a specific, definitive, known objective is held in common by the various stakeholders in a programme (legislators, politicians, administrators, staff, clients/users of a programme, the public or competing sections of the public). Often, however, evaluators have to pressure interested parties, usually administrators, to specify programme objectives. When results are available, one of the interested parties may contend that the 'real' goal of the programme was not studied. For example, was the ambition of a programme to change the behaviour of a number of individuals or to produce a transformation in community climate and responses?[7] What is a means and what is a goal are not always easy to disentangle.

Are unanticipated consequences part of the evaluation of a practice? A programme can be cost-effective but it may endanger the environment. It is a political judgement whether that unexpected outcome should be brought into the evaluation.

The implication of the currently heavy political usage of the term 'unanticipated consequences' (coined by sociologist Robert K. Merton in the 1930s and highlighted in the conservative upsurge of the 1970s) is that the unexpected is usually negative, but that is not always the case. For example, a notable result of many programmes with definitive, limited goals is that one of its most significant outcomes is that it develops the capacities of staff and clients that later enable them to do useful work in other contexts. Should this contribution be included in a cost–benefit calculation?

It is odd to assert that a careful description of policies and, more particularly, of components in a practice is needed. Unfortunately, clearly delineating what a practice does in concrete terms is important when trying to ascertain if it is effective and best. What one person thinks goes on in a practice may differ from what others think. What is central to the effectiveness of a practice may be far from obvious in many situations. What can be modified in a practice without detracting from its effectiveness? Such issues affect the changes of a practice being conducted successfully on a larger or broader scale.

The statistical identification of a 'causal' variable does not explicate the process or mechanisms by which it affects the 'dependent' variable. 'Description' tries to identify what goes on in that black box which actually produces effects.[8]

Careful evaluation of a practice, and possibly its competitors, is expensive and usually requires before, after and after-after data (since the rapid loss of gains – what are termed fade-out effects – may be great). Rigorous evaluations as outlined by Crane (1988) are not easy to structure for they require both experimental and comparison groups that are similar in conditions and outlook.[9] In a valid effort to discover which practice is better, each group would have to undergo a different treatment.

More likely than such experiments are separate evaluations at different times of (possibly) alternative programmes. The assumption is that what was true yesterday is true today, but that may not always be the case.

The general point is that evaluating programmes on the principles of current scientific procedures is expensive and difficult. Many countries lack the conditions and financing for rigorous evaluations which at least approximate experiments. (A political issue that is gathering force in the United States is the deprivation involved in double-blind drug studies that give placebos to patients who might benefit from the drug but who are part of the comparison group.)

New approaches to evaluation are needed. My approach is to distinguish evaluation from before–after estimates, assessment and monitoring. In this formulation, evaluation is restricted to fairly rigorous procedures approximating a full experimental set-up with an appropriate comparison group. As indicated above, such evaluations occur infrequently.

More frequent are before–after measurements of people in a programme without a comparison group or with a rough approximation of one. The hope is that the before–after calculation can be compared with the before–after effects of other programmes with similar objectives and participants.[10] Not all of the benefits or deficiencies measured in the effect stage can be attributed to the programme: a job training programme's effects can be curtailed or expanded by a general rise or fall in unemployment. That is why experimental evaluations are much preferred with adjustments made to factor in the impact of changing conditions on programme effectiveness.

Assessment is less expensive and authoritative but more widely used in judging the effects of a practice. It relies on analysis of data collected by a programme, interviews with staff and users, and the seasoned understanding of experienced persons who know how to appraise practices and programmes. Social scientists may not be the only or best personnel for assessment. In the late 1960s and 1970s the Ford Foundation largely used veteran journalists to report on the effectiveness of programmes. While no comparison with what social scientists might have reported was conducted, the reports were considered useful ways of determining the quality of performance of programmes. Two virtues of using non-social scientists were that reports were presented in a shorter time period and were less expensive than systematic research.

The assessment approach rests on practical knowledge, practical wisdom and implicit benchmarking. Practical knowledge refers not only to information about the problem area and other efforts to deal with it but also involves a sense of how things work 'on the ground', in real-life situations. Practical wisdom refers to the skill or art of asking needed, revealing questions and the seasoned ability to evaluate answers. An example of both practical knowledge and wisdom is to doubt an assertion that 50 per cent of the target population use a service. That would be an unusual accomplishment. Then the question is asked how many people would that be. The answer specifies a number which the assessor knows would overwhelm the service.

Benchmarking refers to setting an appropriate standard of performance. Obviously, that reference goal affects how outcomes are regarded. In the business world the standard is usually set by the performance of the leading organization in that particular endeavour. In the social world that may frequently be too high a goal in light of the constraints facing a programme. The assessor has to specify an appropriate performance level for the various outputs of a programme. That judgement may not appear explicit to the assessor or others.

An obvious drawback of assessment, whether or not conducted by social scientists, is that it is subject to the bias of the assessors. One way of coping with that danger is to deploy more than one independent assessor, preferably with different approaches and perspectives. Another is to insist on the presentation of materials to back up judgements; overall appraisals may be less useful than more detailed analyses.

Monitoring is about checking whether programmes keep to objectives, are making some progress towards their goals and are using their funding in appropriate ways. This is more than an accounting investigation to ensure rectitude in expenditures, though corruption is not a minor issue

A major step in all these efforts, including experiments, is the keeping of better records by a programe, especially the conditions of users at the beginning of the programme. Then it is important to know what activities may have influenced the outcomes for users of the programme. Finally, some after-the-programme effects have to be measured. Unfortunately, it is very difficult to get programme administrators and staff to maintain such records in usable forms.

Clearly, new, inexpensive ways of measuring the accomplishments of programmes are needed. Measures affect outcomes. Goals usually have to be translated into some available data source. What kind of data are collected affects what is regarded as the programme goal as well as how well it meets its goal. For example, psychologists were often the research directors of the individual city projects funded by the US President's Committee on Juvenile Delinquency and Youth Crime in the early 1960s. Their professional training led many of them to use available paper-and-pencil attitude scales to measure programme outcomes, neglecting community or neighbourhood effects which were important in the formulation of programmes.

TRANSFERABILITY

How well does a best practice travel or expand? A best practice is like a plant that is to be transported to a new locale. Can it be dug up without harming it? That is an export problem. What soil, how much sun and water, what attention does it need? That is an import problem – will the practice flourish in new surroundings?

Is the objective to replicate the programme in many other places without modifying its original form (as in the reading programmes discussed in the next section) or is the expectation that the programme has 'adaptive capacity', that it can be changed to work under new circumstances without losing its objectives and achievements? Can the programme work in less stable situations where flexibility is essential?

An export–import problem is that many best practices are developed by a social inventor, entrepreneur or administrator whose charisma is essential to its emergence, prominence, funding and achievement. Can her or his charisma be routinized or embedded in its operations, so that introducing a best practice into another locale or nation, or expanding it, does not damage the programme? New places, new scales produce new problems. Not every programme travels well.[11]

Even where a leader's charisma is not involved in programme achievement, changing locale or expanding scale may cause problems. Economic and cultural conditions, an import problem, affect how a programme works. One approach does not fit all situations. People with different backgrounds or outlooks may respond differently from those initially exposed to the best practice. Expanding a practice to include more locales and people may expose it to dangers of poor administration, inadequate staff, corruption, meddlesome central administrators or attenuated funding.

A best practice should be evaluated in terms of its transferability or replicability. To do that requires different perspectives from those involved in the evaluation of effectiveness. Administrative, political and financial contingencies influence transferability. The peer mentoring and Alcoholics Anonymous cases discussed below offer one approach to promoting transferability.

CASE STUDIES

We turn first to two programmes that emphasize a highly structured, professionalized control. Then we examine two programmes that stress the role of peers.

Professional control   In the spirit of President Johnson's 'war on poverty', the US Congress passed the Elementary and Secondary Education

Act in 1965. This was a major step since education was (and is) primarily a state and local function with little federal funding and less federal supervision. Its Title I provided funding to the states for educational activities to benefit students from low-income, 'disadvantaged' families. The federal appropriations to the states depended on the number of families in the state whose incomes were below the official poverty line. Funding for Title I activities was usually allocated by the states to school districts on the basis of the number of poor children in the district.

Since Congress was reluctant to interfere in school matters that were not regarded as federal issues, few restrictions were placed on the use of the funds. A wide diversity of uses followed. Many of them did not directly benefit children from poor families. Many of them were ill-chosen.

Not surprisingly, overall evaluations of Title I spending showed little gain immediately and considerable fallback later. Within Title I, however, localities have been able to develop effective components. Two widely-used reading programmes for the beginning grades – 'Success for All' and 'Reading One-to-One' – were developed within the Title I framework. Their components and evaluations are discussed by their founders in a case book of effective social programmes (Slavin et al. 1988; Farkas 1988). Jonathan Crane, the exacting editor of the volume, declares that both of them 'have had large effects in evaluation with quasi-experimental designs' and are the closest of the nine programmes studied in this casebook to 'being ready for large-scale application' (Crane 1988: 36).

Each has a rigorous, step-by-step learning procedure for teachers and students. Specific modes of teaching reading – the core requirement for educational achievement – are very detailed. 'Success for All' emphasizes more changes and activities (e.g. family support teams) in the school and community than does 'Reading One-to-One'. Students are tested frequently and students not performing at particular standards are assigned to tutors. In the case of 'Success for All', certified teachers are used as tutors although para-professionals may be used with students with lesser reading problems. 'Reading One-to-One' employs college students, community residents and para-professionals as tutors. Both programmes carefully train and supervise tutors.[12]

What are some of the issues in moving these two well-regarded, perhaps best, practices to a near-universal use in the United States? The present would seem to be a favourable time for institutionalizing successful programmes. Education is regarded as the key to both national and individual long-term economic success. At the same time, the performance of American students lags behind those of other developed nations. This is fertile territory for moving these two well-regarded programmes to near-universal implementation. While their use is growing, they affect only a relatively small number of children. What are some of the issues limiting the spread of the programmes?

In today's era of anti-big government sentiment in the United States it is difficult for the national government to mandate a programme. It may not even be possible to enact national legislation that provides a non-coercive incentive to move to particular modes of operating in schools. In addition, the lobbying of the states and advocates for the poor focus on maintaining the level of funding for Title I, not on the quality of what it does.

Does a 'best practice' have to develop a constituency that will advocate for its use? Does a best practice have to be politically attractive or can strongly positive evaluations successfully carry the message? When do positive evaluations make a practice politically attractive?

A second issue is cost-effectiveness. The Reading One-to-One programme is less expensive than Success for All since the former pays a much lower hourly rate to its non-certified tutors. Assuming no great difference in performance outcomes, then, Reading One-to-One is more cost-effective. But is it more effective than Success for All among the students in great difficulty who need the many facets of this programme? We do not know the answer. (An unfortunate tendency in many evaluations is the offering of overall judgements of outcomes rather than indicating which users are most and least likely to benefit. This is a question of targeting.)

A third issue is: are all components of the two complex programmes needed for success? The overall evaluations do not answer this question. Doing everything that is now done in these programmes would be expensive. This is a question of description and explanation.

A fourth issue is that the programmes have been conducted under the strict supervision of the programme founders. Is the programme appropriate for all schools? Would many school districts relinquish daily operation of their school to outsiders? Can programme quality be maintained if a greatly increased number of school administrators and teachers have to be trained and utilized? In short, how well can the programme travel?

Peer mentoring Peer mentoring is a form of tutoring in which people who share important characteristics with others help them to learn things that they have difficulty in absorbing. The peer mentoring referred to here is of students in higher-grade levels tutoring students in lower grades. What makes them peers is that they are in the same school and differ little in age and grade level. The mentoring students may be volunteers or it may be expected of all students. They may be paid a nominal sum for their work or not at all. In some schools, the expectation is that mentees will become mentors as they move to the next grade levels. In that case, being mentored can be considered an apprenticeship to the stage of becoming a mentor.

Two other forms of mentoring have been studied in the United States: college students or teachers tutoring school students. As far as I have been able to learn, no studies have been conducted to test the relative gains in all three methods. Evaluating the three mentoring methods would require several studies of three experimental groups at the same school level in the same school in the same time period and a control group drawn from that school since school factors could be important. Follow-up studies should be done to compare the fade-out effects of these three approaches. These are not easy conditions to meet.

While a determination of best mentoring practice cannot be made on the basis of well-done evaluations, it is safe to say that peer mentoring has had considerable success. For example, in a low-income, multi-ethnic district in New York City it made a sizeable difference in children's school performance. It has been used with considerable success in schools with upper-middle-class students. The programme has transferability.

The interesting question is why peer mentoring is likely to have very positive outcomes. One important component is the peer quality of the tutoring relationship. The mentor is not a person of authority or judgement but someone who is like the mentee and therefore less forbidding. That leads to a second gain: the mentor is likely to understand the difficulty that the mentee is having in dealing with a learning obstacle; indeed, the mentor may have had a similar experience and be able to address it in language familiar to the mentee.

The transaction between peer mentor and peer mentee has another important result. The peer mentor learns a great deal from the mentoring. Indeed, some important programme designers and advocates like Frank Riessman and Audrey Gartner, co-directors of the Peer Research Laboratory at the City University of New York, conclude that the mentor's gains in understanding are even greater than those of the mentee. That finding should not be a surprise to those of us who have been teachers. Attempting to communicate information to and clarify ideas for students sharpens and deepens instructors' understanding of what they teach. As students, we had few chances to rethink what we had learned in a different setting from that in which we first heard it. (The discussion of peer mentoring is based on conversations with and the articles of Riessman and Gartner.)

A further positive unanticipated consequence is that peer mentoring may contribute to a better school climate. As mentors, students have common experiences that they can discuss, encouraging some academic interest. The school becomes more of a communal learning enterprise as people become mentors and mentees in different fields or at different times. This intervention, then, may have a broad rather than a narrow effect.

What is fundamental to peer mentoring is the discovery and development of an untapped resource – students. Instead of using highly educated resources such as teachers or college students, primary or secondary school students make up an underutilized resource in their schools. Peer mentoring is relatively inexpensive, renewable each year as a new cohort of possible mentors appears for students in lower grades, and adds to rather than subtracts from the resource, the mentor, who is used.

If we cannot declare on the basis of careful comparative evaluations that peer mentoring is the best, most cost-effective mode of tutoring, it is none the less a very effective mode and has been known as such since at least the mid-1960s. It was used and studied then by Mobilization for Youth that conducted a variety of programmes in the Lower East Side of Manhattan and influenced the community action programmes of 'the war on poverty'. This widely-known organization had great success with peer mentoring and circulated its results. It did not become a common practice; presentation is not everything. While peer mentoring is widely used in the United States, its proponents consider it very much underutilized.

Why is that so? The answer lies undoubtedly in the relations between teachers and school administrators, teachers and students and perhaps students and the other two estates. In part, confidence in the ability of students to help other students is low. Certainly, control is important to both administrators and teachers. They may see peer mentoring as a loosening of the reins and an undermining of their roles, as students play an active rather than receiving role in the educational process. Unfamiliarity with how it is done effectively may be important as departures from routine may feel disturbing. The absence of a strong advocacy group at national and local levels also contributes to limited adoption of an effective practice. There is many a slip between the knowledge of a best or highly effective practice and its widespread utilization.

The general significance for non-educational projects of the peer approach is that untapped resources may exist among the people whom programmes aim to help. Rather than regarding them only as objects to be acted upon, they can become subjects who act to improve their situations. That is a major component of the recurrent call for the 'participation' of users in programmes.

Alcoholics Anonymous Alcoholics Anonymous, known as AA, is not a US governmental programme. Nor has it been proven in careful studies in the United States to be more effective than other interventions with confirmed, long-term, chronic alcoholics. (The definition of 'success' is a major question in such evaluations. From conversations with people active in AA, I am convinced that it is a 'best practice' for a large number of alcoholics since they have tried other approaches that failed.) It has made a profound difference for a great many people in many countries. Its approach has been adopted or modified for people suffering other difficulties such as drug addiction or overeating.

The components of its operations warrant examination even if AA lacks certification as a 'best practice'; its parts could be used to move other programmes into a best or better practice. Four components are discussed: the meeting, the 'sponsor' system, AL-ANON, and the centre-chapter organizational mode. It should be added that AA participants may not accept the following formulations which are based on reading AA manuals and discussions over the years with a small number of participants.[13]

In many towns and cities, an AA unit has a regular, frequent (in some localities, daily), usually evening, meeting time. It is attended by active alcoholics and 'recovering' alcoholics (those in AA who abstain from drinking but who are aware of the constant danger that they may drink again). In the meeting, new and veteran members tell of their own difficulties. The session builds on brutal self-honesty. Conversations are first-hand, personal. Participants clarify for themselves what drives them to alcohol, the threats to return to drink in their current mode of living and steps that could be taken to avoid continuing or returning to alcoholism. Involvement with AA is usually not a one-episode experience; people continue to participate over many years, if not for the rest of their lives.

The AA meeting is clearly a peer process although it does not involve a direct mentoring activity. Professional counsellors are not talking to alcoholics; alcoholics are. That first-hand knowledge is crucial, for it promotes the rapid identification of the many ways of denying one's alcoholism and of the many manoeuvres that maintain it. Those who have been through the turmoil of alcoholism – abstinence, sliding back into alcoholism, recovery, failure, recovery – speak authoritatively and clearly about what they are experiencing. Their personal testimonies are easier to take and follow; they have the ring of authenticity and testify to the fact that others have been able to surmount the pain of giving up a crutch.

The general theme at an AA meeting is to avoid advice-giving and confrontation, and only to offer personal accounts that may be helpful to others. The professional stance of 'Let me tell you what is wrong and what to do about it' is absent. The term 'recovering alcoholic' implies that the now-abstainer is always in danger of returning to drinking and is not in a privileged position *vis-à-vis* the current alcoholic. That outlook does not mean that professional help – such as in a residential, 'drying out' clinic – is discouraged.

A second feature is the 'sponsor' system. A new member becomes associated with an existing member. The new member can call on his or her sponsor for help and, indeed, the sponsor will respond to a call for help at any time of day or night. The sponsor system, another form of peer relationship, is based on mutuality. Both sponsor and sponsored benefit from the relationship: feeling understood and getting aid are important when staying sober or recovering from an alcoholic bout; understanding others is important for understanding oneself; accepting a responsibility for another strengthens one. These are all elements in the peer gain.

Third, the AA approach is comprehensive in that intimates and partners of those in AA can join a sister organization. AL-ANON began in the early days of AA when the wives of the two AA founders met independently to discuss the difficulties that they experienced living

with their alcoholic mates. As AA grew so did AL-ANON. Its members
are the spouses, relatives and other relational partners of those in AA.
It has two effects: it helps the partner learn how to cope with the other's
alcoholism and its attendant behaviour – backsliding, deception, stealing,
anger – and it helps the alcoholic as the partner has a greater understanding of what is happening. Again, the peer, mutual-benefit quality
is important: partners talk with other partners about their experiences
and feelings. The double benefit of helping both the partner and the
alcoholic emerges from the peer contact. I do not know of any evaluations of AL-ANON but, again, many participants testify to the great
benefits of understanding and strengthened self-confidence.

Fourth, the mode of organization of Alcoholics Anonymous is an
extraordinary accomplishment. It is self-financing, not dependent on
sales to non-members or support from outside, unlike many organizations which are dependent in one way or another on their relations with
non-members. It combines clear, firm rules at the centre with high
discretion in the units or local chapters. Bureaucratic incrustations are
avoided. The centre is somewhat self-financing through the sale of
publications and materials but needs donations from chapters. The
central staff is small for an organization involving millions of people.
Because of problems of bureaucracy and corruption in many programmes designed for the poor, it offers many leads when rethinking
administration.

The rules for the local chapters are few and specified. The basic
tenets of AA are codified in its famous 'Twelve Steps' but no one is
punished for transgression. Business transactions cannot be conducted
among the members (although surreptitiously that is done). The chapters
conduct their affairs on their own, making arrangements for where and
when they meet. Chapter costs are very small and usually only those of
renting a meeting space and placing notices so that people know of the
meeting. Little money is contributed to the central office.

The genius of the arrangement lies in the combination of a central
normative position and high chapter autonomy. The mode of operation
is mainly set by the rules as developed by the founders in 1935. They
are seldom modified or changed so that a sharply defined framework
for the chapters has long been in place. Within that framework, the
chapters have wide autonomy: a central, unifying set of prescriptions
with untrammelled chapter discretion. This arrangement may not work
in many circumstances as it has for AA worldwide but it offers great

possibilities in others. It offers universal principles and varied practices and adaptations.[14] Its principles are used in many different kinds of twelve-step groups.

AA exists in more than 100 countries – a formidable accomplishment. Furthermore, the approach has been adapted to deal with many other problems and ailments, again in many nations. It certainly travels well. AA-type peer groups have been formed to deal with addiction to violence, drug-use, overeating as well as coping with physical ailments. Each group shares a common problem and its members come together to discuss and benefit from their experiences. In the case of people with physical problems, the group has been able to influence the behaviour and practices of the professional caretakers, physicians and nurses. Occasionally, professionals regard the peer group as a component of the treatment process and they have sometimes modified their practices as a result of the issues raised by the peer group.

Many public and non-profit programmes depend on some form of peer or buddy influence. For example, in many military units what motivates soldiers to bravery is not patriotism or anger at the enemy but their relationship to a peer, a buddy or buddies in their unit. Frequently, a military command consciously and sometimes openly seeks to build a buddy system in order to inspire an esprit de corps.

Connections are the motivators to positive action (Miller and Striver 1997). Awareness of this influence could lead to more effective use of it.

THE MESSAGE

Perhaps the most general point is that the implementation or administration or management of a programme is crucially important. Programme design has to consider ways to induce competent implementation. Adaptation and flexibility within bounds are important.

A second point is that frequent (but not too frequent) monitoring and assessment can be an aid. These two procedures should not be regarded only as success–fail or stop-or-go decisions but as ways of providing leads on how to improve programmes. This will probably involve more collaborative relationships between programmes and assessors.

Many discussions of best practices, if not under that name, emphasize the importance of comprehensiveness and integration. To be effective an intervention may have to span a variety of relationships. UK Prime

Minister Tony Blair uses the phrases 'joined up-problems' requiring 'joined-up solutions'. An example is the US pre-school programme 'Head Start' which began with a medical and dental check-up of the children in it. Unfortunately, Head Start did not do anything initially to connect the children to health facilities that could deal with any health difficulties that were uncovered, a failure of comprehensiveness. A Head Start programme was not often built upon by the schools that its students entered. This failure of integration of pre-school and school activity contributed to the fade-out of much of the positive gains initially exhibited by students in the Head Start programme.[15]

An excellent practice does not stand alone; its relationships with households, community, and other institutions and programmes are crucial.

Seldom can a best practice be taken over in its original form and implemented successfully in new circumstances and/or on a bigger scale. Changing circumstances and scale changes practices if only because new and additional administrators and staff must join the practice. A less-than-best practice can be made highly effective with a top-notch, dedicated administrator and staff. Unfortunately, it is also true that a best practice can be decimated by a poor administration or staff or by uncertain funding. While a practice influences staff, staff influences practice.

What peer-oriented efforts suggest is how to conduct programmes. They point to the importance of recognizing and realizing the capacities and potential capacities of those whom they seek to help. Understanding the poor and building on their strengths leads to effective programmes. Simply stated, involvement from the 'target' population is an effective way to conduct a programme. Support for and effectiveness of programmes are largely based on the quality of the relationships that are developed with and among the important influences on a practice, that is users, staff, administrators, funders and politicians. It is important to recognize and respond to all these influences.

Peer programmes have the merit of relative low cost or, in the case of peer mentoring, virtually no cost. That quality can be a danger, for the peer model may be primarily used to reduce costs. That outlook is likely to corrupt and distort programmes from their primary objective of involving people in their own development. Peer programmes cannot be simply willed into life without responsiveness to the people involved. For then, the programme will appear an imposition, a low-quality effort.

Peer efforts should be used as components of programmes, as ways of improving the performance of programmes. They are not substitutes for the variety of aids that poor people need; they are ways of improving some of these aids. Peer components are built on respect for the participants, not on cost-saving.

Perhaps the most important point about the transfer of programmes is that a practice should not be regarded as a hardy cactus plant that can be moved to almost any place and still thrive. A practice has to be adapted to its new conditions and relationships. The important promise of 'best practices' is that they may stir political action to utilize ways of operating that are known to be highly productive and can be suited to local circumstances.

NOTES

I am indebted to Audrey Gartner for editorial and substantive advice.

1. Miller et al. (1982); Miller (1987); Miller and Rein (1967); Rein (1970).

2. The term 'best practices' may be interpreted in at least two ways. One understanding is that it refers to a programme that is more effective than other programmes with the same objective. A second view is looser and refers not only to a programme but also includes components of programmes that perform better than competitor parts in other programmes. The latter view is mainly adopted here although policy, programme, practice and component are not sharply delineated. 'Practice' can refer to a programme as well as to a component.

3. See the President's Initiative on Race (1999), esp. pp. viii–ix which outline key goals and questions in determining 'promising practices'; and the National Conference for Community and Justice (1999).

4. In the Republic of Ireland, the Combat Poverty Agency, a quasi-independent governmental unit led by Hugh Frazer, plays a key role in 'poverty proofing' proposals and policies.

5. Lieberson (1998: 177–91). A brief but pointed critique of methods rather than Lieberson's questioning of statistical inferences is Rainwater (1986: 194–201). Nobel Prize-winner Robert Solow points out that 'small effects' are the likely outcome of evaluations of experiments. Their prevalence 'opens the way to alternative interpretations of the research findings' (Solow 1986: 219–20).

6. Two excellent accounts of issues in evaluation and social experimentation are Crane (1998: 1–42) and Haveman (1986: 586–605). A useful book that does not focus on the pitfalls of research is Schorr with Schorr (1988). Schorr (1997) is even more useful and emphasizes what can be done nationally on the basis of actual programmes.

7. A thoughtful analysis of the problems of evaluation can be found in chs 4 and 5 of Schorr (1997).

8. Cf. Rainwater (1986: 199–200).

9. The emergence of the term 'comparison group' acknowledges the difficulties of obtaining a true 'control group' that matches exactly the experimental group except for the impact of the intervention that is to be evaluated.

10. Most of the time comparison with other programmes with similar objectives is not possible because of financial or political unwillingness to try out different programmes.

11. A leading American business executive asserts that he prefers a 75 per cent idea executed 100 per cent, over a 100 per cent idea executed at 75 per cent. Implementation may be more compelling than creativity.

12. A redent laudatory report on 'Success for All' is Bulkeley (1999). This account downplays the importance of tutoring and emphasizes the requirement that 80 per cent of the teachers in the school that the journalist visited had to agree to the introduction of 'Success for All' and its intrusive supervision. Teacher support is sought in order to ensure co-operation with the programme which stresses strict and highly specific procedures.

13. I am particularly grateful for the comments of Ray Stiver who saved me from some of my errors in describing AA.

14. The foregoing interpretation of AA ignores what many members consider a crucial component of its effectiveness – confidence in the beneficence of a 'Higher Power' (or 'force' for those who are not religious believers). My rationalism resists grappling with that perspective.

15. This has not been true of high-quality pre-school programmes. See Schweihart and Weikart (1998).

REFERENCES

Bulkeley, William M. (1999) 'Teacher's Pet: Now Johnny Can Read if Teacher Just Keeps Doing What He's Told', *Wall Street Journal*, 19 July, pp. A1, A9.

Crane, Jonathan (1998) 'Building on Success', in J. Crane (ed.), *Social Programs That Work* (New York: Russell Sage Foundation).

Farkas, George (1998) '"Reading One-to-One": An Intensive Program Serving a Great Many Students While Still Achieving Large Effects', in J. Crane (ed.), *Social Programs That Work* (New York: Russell Sage Foundation).

Haveman, Robert H. (1986) 'Social "Experimentation" and Social Experimentation', *Journal of Human Resources*, Vol. 21, no. 4, pp. 586–605; reprinted as no. 557 in the IRP Reprint Series of the Institute for Research on Poverty, University of Wisconsin-Madison.

Lieberson, Stanley (1998) 'Examples, Submerged Statements and the Neglected Applications of Philosophy to Social Theory', in Alan Sica (ed.), *What is Social Theory?* (Oxford: Basil Blackwell).

Miller, Jean Baker and Irene Striver (1997) *The Healing Connection* (Boston: Beacon Press).

Miller, S. M. (1987) 'Evaluation as Lesson-drawing', in Bernadette Barry and Mary Whelan (eds), *Evaluate It* (Dublin: Combat Poverty Agency).

Miller, S. M. and Martin Rein (1967) 'The Demonstration Project as a Strategy of

Change', in Mayer Zald (ed.), *Organizing for Community Welfare* (Chicago: Quadrangle Books).

Miller, S. M., Barbara Tomaskovic-Devey and Donald Tomaskovic-Devey (1982) 'Pilot and Demonstration Projects as Political Events', in Sr. Stanislaus Kennedy (ed.), *Poverty in Ireland* (Dublin: Combat Poverty Agency).

National Conference for Comunity and Justice (1999) *Intergroup Relations in the United States: Seven Promising Practices* (New York).

President's Initiative on Race, The (1999) *Pathways to One America in the 21st Century: Promising Practices for Racial Reconciliation* (Washington DC, January).

Rainwater, Lee (1986) 'A Sociologist's View of the Income Maintenance Experiments', in Alicia H. Munnell (ed.), *Lessons from the Income Maintenance Experiments* (Washington DC: Federal Reserve Bank of Boston and Brookings Institution).

Rein, Martin (1970) *Social Policy: Issues of Choice and Change* (New York: Random House).

Rice, E. B. (1974) *Extension in the Andes: An Evaluation of Official US Assistance to Agricultural Extension Services in Central and South America* (Cambridge, MA: MIT Press); originally published as 'Evaluation Paper 74' by the US Agency for International Development, 1971.

Schorr, Lisbeth B. (1997) *Common Purpose: Strengthening Families and Neighborhoods to Rebuild America* (New York: Doubleday).

Schorr, Lisbeth B. with Daniel Schorr (1988) *Within Our Reach: Breaking the Cycle of Disadvantage* (New York: Doubleday).

Schweihart, Lawrence J. and David P. Weikart (1998) 'High/Scope Perry Preschool Effects at Age Twenty-seven', in J. Crane (ed.), *Social Programs That Work* (New York: Russell Sage Foundation).

Slavin, Robert E. et al. (1998) 'Success for All: Achievement Outcomes of a Schoolwide Reform Model', in J. Crane (ed.), *Social Programs That Work* (New York: Russell Sage Foundation).

Solow, Martin (1986) 'An Economist's View of the Income Maintenance Experiments', in Alicia H. Munnell (ed.), *Lessons from the Income Maintenance Experiments* (Washington DC: Federal Reserve Bank of Boston and Brookings Institution).

FOUR

Some Methodological Issues in Determining Good Practices in Social Policy: The Case of High-achieving Countries

SANTOSH MEHROTRA

• This chapter discusses some methodological issues about 'best practices' in the context of so-called high-achieving countries that have high levels of health and education indicators for their level of income. In every developing region there are countries that have made significant improvements in their non-income human development indicators: Costa Rica, Cuba and Barbados in Latin America and the Caribbean, Botswana, Mauritius and Zimbabwe in Sub-Saharan Africa, Kerala and Sri Lanka in South Asia, and Republic of Korea and Malaysia in East Asia (Mehrotra and Jolly 1997).

This chapter attempts to address the following questions: How can high-achieving countries be identified? What criteria are used and why? It elaborates on the content of the longitudinal studies we did in these countries, and why we examined the issues chosen. It asks: What is the optimal context for a good practice? And offers some thoughts about the replicability of good practices. Finally, it examines how the historical approach we used in these country studies can be replicated by others (i.e. not the policy lessons from these countries for other developing countries, but the analytical approach used in studying them).

THE CRITERIA FOR CHOICE OF HIGH-ACHIEVING COUNTRIES

The research began with an attempt to identify countries which could be regarded as 'high achievers'. In other words, methodologically, we began with a purposive sample, not a random sample, since our objective was to understand why and how some countries became high achievers.

This required a conceptual framework within which the notion of 'high achievers' could be understood.

A rate of per capita income growth could possibly be one axis of high achievement, given that income growth makes it possible for humans to improve their overall well-being. However, consistent with the notion of human development, we chose the first two of the three elements which make up (with equal weight) the human development index (HDI): longevity, knowledge and income. It is important here to emphasize that we were interested in all three aspects.

More importantly, high achievement was not defined in terms of *all* aspects of human development. The notion of human development or capabilities also incorporates the concepts of civil and political liberties and the freedom of individuals to participate in community or state decisions. These aspects of human development were deliberately not part of the study design, for a variety of reasons. It is much more difficult to rank countries according to universally acceptable criteria of civil and political liberties. In fact, when the Human Development Report tried to do so in the early 1990s it generated much controversy.

It is common knowledge that health and education indicators tend to be highly correlated with income per capita. However, that does not establish whether the causality goes from healthy, educated individuals earning higher incomes, or that growing incomes enable people and states to provide better health and education services. In any case, it is useful to establish whether a country has health and education indicators higher or lower than those found for other countries in the same income range – implying that policy makes a difference, even though level of income may be one determinant of health and education status.

We were also interested in a cross-regional spread in our purposive sample. So the countries chosen were not high achievers in respect of the selected indicators in an absolute sense, but relative to other countries in their region. In other words, it was not important to compare country indicators across regions in terms of the level of a particular indicator, e.g. Zimbabwe with Cuba, but only with countries in their region.

We also relied on qualitative information and previous research to arrive at the choice of countries. This led to a choice of countries which were already fairly well known in and outside their region as having done exceptionally well on certain social indicators, e.g. Costa Rica, Kerala state in India, and Sri Lanka. For the others the choice of countries was more formal.

The indicators we began by looking at were outcome indicators: life expectancy and literacy rates. These indicators were better in the selected countries for the early 1990s when compared to the regional average. For major health indicators of a population, the selected countries have better outcome indicators than all countries in the region, i.e. for life expectancy at birth, under-five mortality rate (U5MR), infant-mortality rate (IMR), and maternal mortality rate (MMR). The same holds true of adult literacy rates in 1970 and 1990. Clearly there are other countries for which some indicators are higher than the regional average, but we found that for the chosen countries they were consistently better than the regional average for most sectors.

Superior outcome indicators are usually based on, or determined by, better than normal output or process indicators. When one delves deeper, beyond the outcome indicators, and begins to examine the output indicators (e.g. immunization rate, access to safe water and sanitation, doctor to population ratio, nurse to population ratio, hospital bed to population ratio), the same holds true.

Data of a detailed nature, especially on output and process indicators (e.g. percentage of low-weight births as a determinant of child nutritional status, percentage of primary school children completing five years of schooling), are not easily available internationally. Hence, national studies by national researchers were necessary in order to mine historical sources of data.

We compared the rate of change of selected outcome and output indicators (for which data were available) among the ten countries chosen and the rest of the developing countries, i.e. a total of 124 countries. The percentage change in U5MR and primary gross enrolment ratio (GER) for both males and females between 1960 and 1990 was used; in addition, the percentage change in literacy rates for females and males between 1970 and 1990 was used. This comparison of the percentage change in the ten selected countries with all other countries revealed that the rate of improvement in our set was higher for all variables (except primary enrolment for males), and this difference was statistically significant.

The oil-rich countries were deliberately excluded from the purposive sample of high achievers, with the intention of removing a source of bias in our analysis. Most oil-rich countries in the Middle East have also been able, within the last quarter century, to use their gains from rising oil prices to provide widespread access to health and education services for their population, and have improved their social indicators enormously. Thus, between 1960 and 1991, the U5MR fell in Saudi Arabia from 292 to 43, in the United Arab Emirates from 239 to 29, in Oman from 278 to 42, and in Iran from 233 to 62 (UNICEF 1993). However, these countries were excluded from the high achievers precisely on account of the windfall nature of the rents accruing to these countries in the 1970s and 1980s. In other words, countries with such windfall gains in income per capita are anticipated to experience improvements in social outcomes, unless government policies are particularly perverse.[1] In choosing 'high achievers', we needed to be sure that countries were starting from a level playing field – to the extent such a thing exists in social science.

THE CONTENT OF THE LONGITUDINAL STUDIES

The studies were mainly concerned with health and educational outcomes – why and how those outcomes became possible at a rate faster than that achieved by other developing countries.

Almost half the existing disease burden in the world comes from communicable or infectious diseases, poor nutrition, and maternal and peri-natal causes. Under-fives are particularly vulnerable and suffer from high-mortality risk. Thus, the national studies were especially concerned with the fate of children in the society, and that of their mothers, over a thirty- to forty-year period, depending upon the period of the health transition (subject to availability of data). In 1891 in England and Wales (when its age distribution was bell-shaped), children under five constituted only about 12 per cent of the population, but they accounted for over 35 per cent of total deaths. In 1955 in Latin America and the Caribbean, under-fives were below 18 per cent of the population, but accounted for over 45 per cent of the total deaths. To a large extent life expectancy figures in a society are driven by the U5MR.

Demographers point out that a health transition or change in disease pattern occurs in two steps. First, a demographic transition, when mortality from communicable diseases falls, and, partly as a result, fertility falls as well. As fertility declines, and non-communicable diseases become more important as a cause of death (i.e. an epidemiological or health transition), the population grows older. More infants and under-fives survive, and the age-structure of the population changes from being bell-shaped to rectangular.

Prima facie evidence for the selected countries seemed to suggest that this health transition (though not necessarily the demographic transition in all cases) was either well advanced or fairly advanced in the 1990s, and the objective was to understand why and how this was achieved relatively rapidly. If the health and demographic transition is to be hastened, the health system in developing countries has to be structured in response to the pattern of disease. Although all developing countries have invested heavily in health, in most countries the facilities and equipment as well as human resources are skewed in favour of the top of the health system pyramid – the specialized, urban-based referral hospital, as opposed to health centres and district hospitals to serve the preventive health and basic curative care needs of the population. The latter would address most cost-effectively the disease pattern in developing countries. So the question facing the national researchers was whether the health infrastructure and pattern of human resource development in high-achieving countries is different from that of most developing countries.

Almost half of the preventable deaths of under-fives in poor countries are the result of diarrhoeal and respiratory illness, exacerbated by malnutrition – all of which are most cost-effectively dealt with through preventive measures at lower-level facilities. But in some developing countries a single teaching hospital at the top of the pyramid can take 20 per cent or more of the government's health budget. This leads to both inefficiency and inequity.

The longitudinal studies for each of the selected countries were required to address some of these important issues relating to health inputs and outputs that underlie the health problems in most developing countries. First, in regard to investment in health infrastructure and equipment, how did policy ensure that urban bias in the distribution of facilities, which existed at the beginning of the period, was removed? Second, how was the imbalance in human resources which existed at the time of independence between rural and urban health services and primary and tertiary care addressed? Third, what kind of mother and child programmes were organized within a system of primary health care (PHC)? And finally, how significant were interventions in (i) safe drinking water and sanitation, and (ii) nutrition seen to be in improvements in health outcomes? We were interested also in determining the progress made so far towards a demographic transition.

Apart from a qualitative analysis of the health services that such questions entailed, and the policies that determined the quality of services, the national studies also attempted to examine input, process and output indicators relevant to each question. For the distribution of infrastructure, it is possible to look for hospital bed per 1000 population, or the population covered by a primary health centre – particularly the evolution of such indicators over time. For human resources, it is important to examine not merely the physician or nurse per 1000 population, but the distribution between rural and urban areas. Since there has been a massive expansion in many developing countries of physician training at public expense, the nurse-to-physician ratio is a critical determinant of the efficiency of the outreach of PHC services. It is equally useful to find out how the normal developing country staffing problem in the government sector – covert or overt refusal of staff to serve in rural areas – was resolved. As regards water and sanitation, the common problem in developing countries has been that while states are responsive to a vocal urban elite's demands for clean water and piped sewerage in towns and cities, the peri-urban and rural areas get neglected, or have to provide for themselves. Those are precisely the areas where the outreach of PHC services is poor, forcing the population to rely on unregulated private providers.

Underlying the questions (discussed above) was the fact that at the end of the 1970s a consensus had emerged among health specialists about the principles of PHC underlined in the declaration of Alma Ata.[2] What is that consensus? Before the 1930s the contribution of medical technology was limited.[3] Since the introduction of anti-bacterial drugs and new vaccines in the 1930s many potent interventions against infectious diseases have been available. One principle underlying the Alma Ata declaration is that it is necessary to overtake the lag between the discovery of modern medical knowledge and its use in the setting of the community. But the effect of medical innovations on health have depended upon other variables, among them incomes of the poor, improved schooling, and the effect on health systems of public policies. Thus a second principle of the declaration is that a vertical medical system is not really effective unless it is integrated with other activities in the society in a joint attack on the problems of development. Health is not simply a 'sector', a responsibility of the health ministry alone; it must be an explicit goal to be achieved through all sectors with mass participation of the citizens – through education, better nutrition, and national and local community leadership. A third principle is that successful health organization implies reliance on cost-effective strategies for serving the entire population rather than only the well-off. However, the majority of developing countries have examples of major hospitals whose operational costs resulted in the curtailment of health clinics and preventive services.

The fact is that while the majority of countries have, since the Alma Ata declaration, paid lip-service to promoting PHC (e.g. millions of village health workers have been trained but left to their own devices), the majority of health resources are still not applied to achieving it. On the other hand, most of the selected countries applied the principles long before these principles were enshrined in the Alma Ata declaration. The recent declines in mortality in the post-colonial world have been much greater than the declines in the now-industrialized countries in the 100 years up to the mid-twentieth century, since they did not have to wait for the slow, evolutionary pace of medical discoveries and their application to the majority of the population. But the selected countries managed to achieve even quicker declines precisely by applying the Alma Ata principles in practice.

The focus of the analysis in the education sector was almost entirely on primary and secondary education. This was so for two main reasons. First, it is well known that the social rate of return is highest for primary, followed by secondary education, and the social rate of return for higher education is the lowest (World Bank 1995). Second, it is also well known that primary and secondary education have high health benefits for society.

The quantitative and qualitative aspects of the achievement of universal primary education in the selected countries, as well as the policies which made it possible, were examined. These countries had universalized primary education long before most of the rest of the developing countries in their region. On the quantitative side, we were interested in understanding how gross/net enrolment rates of 100 or near 100 per cent were achieved, when the majority of developing countries are still far from the Education for All goal at the beginning of the twenty-first century.

Another critical aspect of the effectiveness of the education system that was examined was the primary completion rate. Without completing at least four years of primary education, it is unlikely that children can remain literate, and will indeed lose the skills acquired very quickly. Also, it is well known that drop-outs at the primary or early secondary stage normally join the millions of child labourers, so common in South

Asia, Africa and Latin America (Grootaert and Kanbur 1994; Siddiqui and Patrinos 1995).

In fact, quantitative expansion of enrolment has been seen for so long as a primary goal that quality of education has been at a discount. The approach to universalizing primary education was: 'Let us ensure that all children are enrolled, and the quality of education can be taken care of later.' The outcome of such dichotomous thinking has been huge wastage in the form of repetition and drop-out. The selected countries, however, had managed to minimize this wastage – and it was critical to understand how the quantity–quality 'trade-off' was managed by these countries.

A cross-cutting issue, underlying all the analysis of the quantitative expansion of school education, was gender equity. For most developing countries there are very substantial gender differences in every education indicator, with ramifications not only for the health of all and the productivity of women (and thus their capacity to earn independent and higher incomes), but also with major implications for hastening the demographic transition.

The analysis of resource allocation for the health and education sector lay at the heart of the longitudinal studies of each selected country. It was essential to build long-term trends of level equity and efficiency of public spending in the health and education sectors. It was usually not too difficult to determine the inter-sectoral allocation to the health and education sectors as a whole. In the education sector, it was not overly difficult to find data for intra-sectoral allocation by level of education – primary, secondary and tertiary. Comparisons were made, where possible, of the macro-economic priority (e.g. health expenditure to GDP ratio) and fiscal priority (health expenditure as a share of total government expenditure) of sectoral allocations. Even more important was the analysis of per capita sectoral expenditure trends.

A question that was equally relevant was the degree to which the health and education services required out-of-pocket expenditures for the family. For poor families, a sudden medical expense can make the difference between a family being below or above the poverty line in a given year. For poor families, having to make a decision whether to send, say, all four children to school, or send the oldest to work after two or three years of schooling so that the rest can continue in school, is an almost daily occurrence. When faced with a school-related out-of-pocket expense, the poor family will decide to send the boy to school, while withdrawing the girl – a major determinant of the unequal gender outcomes in education noted earlier.

Finally, apart from the financing (public or private) of services, a question that was also examined was the public–private mix in the delivery of services.

THE OPTIMAL CONTEXT FOR A GOOD PRACTICE

The historical analysis of the high-achieving countries revealed some common elements in social and economic policy, or best practices. The objective of identifying best practices clearly derives from the assumption that these countries followed policies that were different from those of the rest, and hence there may be lessons from their policies for other countries. This section begins by briefly summarizing those principles of good social policy that seemed to be common to the high achievers (before we can discuss, in more methodological terms, what the optimal context for a good practice might be).

The first principle we noted is the pre-eminent role of public action, regardless of whether it was a centrally planned economy or a market economy. The experience of the industrialized countries from a comparable period of development offers the same insight. The second was that while the level of social spending matters for health and education outcomes, the equity of the intra-sectoral spending pattern matters even more.[4] The social investment was also protected during times of economic crisis as well as structural adjustment. The third was that efficiency in the utilization of human and financial resources needs to be practised if social spending is not to become a burden on the state exchequer. A number of specific good practices in both health and education sectors ensured both allocative and technical efficiency in resource use. The fourth was that there seemed to be a sequence of social investment: educational achievement preceded, or was simultaneous with the introduction of health interventions. This ensured that health services were effectively used when made available. Finally, women were equal agents of change, and not mere beneficiaries of a welfare state. Underlying each of these principles were specific good practices of social policy (Mehrotra and Jolly 1997: chs 2 and 3).

An over-arching common principle which underlay the development strategy in the high-achieving countries seems to have been that they did not give overwhelming or exclusive priority to achieving economic growth, or macro-economic stability first, while keeping social development in abeyance.[5] The high achievers demonstrate that it is possible for countries to relieve the non-income dimensions of poverty, and achieve social indicators comparable to those of industrialized countries, notwithstanding the level of income. The poor should not have to wait for the benefits of growth. On the other hand, for the Washington consensus, per capita income growth is a predominant part of the strategy since they believe 'there is no general tendency for distribution to worsen with growth' and that 'distribution remains stable over long periods of time' (Deininger and Squire 1996).

We found that the social dimensions of poverty were relieved in the selected countries for almost the entire population. However, except in a minority of countries (Cuba, Mauritius, Korea and Malaysia) income-poverty remained more stubborn, although it certainly declined in most of them. Where income-poverty has been resistant, the pace of economic growth has been relatively slow.

Based on the historical analysis of the high-achieving countries, is it possible to establish whether there are certain key conditions or an optimal context for success in social development? In all the selected countries there were specific, nationally determined forces particular to the country in question which led to policies favourable to health and education development. However, some common themes did emerge in a detailed analysis of the country cases. Some tentative observations are possible.

One common theme as regards the context that emerged was that there existed in each society a mechanism for the articulation of 'voice', in a macro, societal sense. The role of ideology and politics cannot be ignored as driving forces behind public action in the selected countries. Thus, in Cuba, as in all other developing centrally planned economies (Vietnam is another good example), communist ideology was the driving force behind state action not only in reducing poverty, but also in providing equitable access to health and education services to all. In Kerala, the process began during colonial times in the independent royal state of Travancore-Cochin, partly by the local king in response to missionary activity. After independence, however, which is when most of the social development occurred, the process was driven by the competitive electoral politics between the Communist Party and the populist Congress Party. In Sri Lanka, competitive electoral democracy allowed the societal consensus around a dominant socialist ideology, underscored by strong Buddhist influences, to be expressed in the form of social interventions. Health interventions soon after independence followed close on the heels of the spread of universal primary schooling.

Competive electoral politics seems to have played a role elsewhere as well. In Costa Rica the context for public intermediation was provided by an essentially social-democratic consensus in a democracy which has lasted almost 150 years, with elections every four years. The existence of such a strong tradition of electoral democracy stands in strong contrast to the rest of Latin America. Similarly, in the island states of Mauritius and Barbados, it was competitive electoral politics which drove the state's interest in health and education services. Both island states have a tradition of electoral democracy based on the parliamentary system.

Likewise, Botswana's political history since independence has been rather exceptional by African standards (Duncan et al. 1997). As in other African countries, independence was preceded by a multi-party election and western-style constitution, but it is more unusual that these are retained after that time. The political process in Botswana has been for the most part democratic, with regular free elections and a range of political parties both within and outside parliament.[6] In Zimbabwe, the vehicle of 'voice' was the liberation struggle. Social development came more as a natural consequence of the liberation struggle; and the country maintained a reasonably strong democratic framework within a one-party dominant state. During the liberation struggle, new forms of social organization emerged that encouraged popular participation under the auspices of the liberation movements. After independence popular participation was mobilized and channelled by party and central-government programmes and structures.[7]

Thus, in seven of the ten cases (the exceptions being Cuba, Korea and possibly Malaysia) there seems to be a clear tradition of a democratic system, with a multi-party system and predictably frequent and fair elections. Cuba is a one-party state, and Korea and Malaysia have been one-party-dominant states. But even in Cuba and Malaysia there has been scope for 'voice' in the governance process. In Malaysia social development was the outcome of the state's attempt to correct the social and economic disadvantage of the Malay population based on ethnicity. The dominant political party in Malaysia has indeed governed through a coalition of parties, the other parties being essentially representative of the two other major ethnic groups (Chinese and Indian).[8] In other words, in all states except Korea voice in governance was a key element of success.[9]

As distinct from the form of popular representation, there is the question as to whether a particular structure of the organization of production is a necessary condition, or the optimal context for ensuring longevity and knowledge for the majority of the population. It is noticeable that only one high achiever was a centrally planned economy: Cuba. Of course, there are other developing countries with a centrally planned economy that have achieved health and education levels far superior to those achieved by developing market economies at the same level of per capita income, e.g. Vietnam, Mongolia and the Central Asian states during the Soviet period. In fact, given the small number of developing countries in the post-war, post-colonial period that have been centrally planned, it is remarkable that such a high proportion of them managed to achieve social indicators well above those for other countries in the same income bracket.[10] However, the point here is that the rest of the selected high achievers were all market economies. Given that the vast majority of developing market economies in their region were unable to match this improvement of social indicators, the lessons from the high achievers become particularly salient for these market economies. In fact, methodologically, our arguments are strengthened by the fact that all but one of the selected countries were market economies (rather than centrally planned). It reinforces the case for replicability – if it can be done in nine, it can be done elsewhere.

In determining the optimal context, a critical issue is whether economic growth is a necessary condition of social investment. We have already discussed above that all the selected countries made substantial improvements in their health and education indicators early in their development process, when incomes were still low. All started as low-income countries; while some have graduated to become middle-income countries, many of them (Cuba, Zimbabwe, Kerala, Sri Lanka) have remained low-income countries, having experienced limited economic growth. Yet they managed to make major improvements in the health and education indicators of their population and, as we have seen, they have life expectancy and literacy rates in some cases comparable to those found in industrialized countries. Clearly, an optimal context for social investment is not necessarily a prior record of rapid income growth.

However, although quantitative indicators of health and education status have not been affected adversely, the quality of services does seem to have been affected by slow economic growth. Thus relative economic stagnation – in Sri Lanka, Kerala, Zimbabwe and (in the 1990s) Cuba – has created problems for the social sectors. In Sri Lanka, food subsidies and free health and education services were made possible by heavy taxation of export plantation crops – tea, rubber and coconut. Although international commodity prices dipped in the late 1950s and 1960s, on account of the political difficulty of cutting social expenditures and the food subsidy, the government continued to tax heavily the plantation sector, and jeopardized the plantation industry (Alailama and Sanderatne 1997). Quite clearly, the economy needs to generate a surplus for social investment, but excessive surplus extraction may lead to lower economic growth ultimately causing a curtailment of social expenditures.

Kerala offers similar lessons, though for rather different reason. Kerala ranks low (ninth) among the twenty-five states of India in terms of per capita income and has had one of the lowest levels of industrialization. The overall result is that the economy has been practically stagnant since 1975 (Krishnan 1997). The scope for increasing public expenditure in order to improve quality of services has been limited by slow growth.

Similarly, Zimbabwe's per capita income growth was slightly negative (0.2 per cent) over the 1980s. Hence the concern in the 1990s shifted from the social policy, distribution and equity concerns which dominated Zimbabwe in the 1980s to aggregate growth and balance-of-payments concerns. There has been a rise in IMR and maternal mortality as real health expenditures shrank and fees were introduced at health services (Loewenson and Chisvo 1997). Clearly, then, sustained improvements in the quality of services will require increased per capita expenditures, especially if the population is still growing. Increased per capita social expenditures, whether private or public, may be difficult to sustain in the absence of per capita income growth.

On a more methodological note, it is worth noting that some of these conclusions, tentative though they might be, might not have been possible unless the number of countries (i.e. observations) was reasonable. In other words, there are at least three countries (Korea, Malaysia, Mauritius) that managed to combine economic growth with poverty-reduction *and* social development. Similarly, there are four cases (of the ten) that did not manage to combine rapid economic growth with social development (Kerala, Sri Lanka, Zimbabwe, Cuba), or sustain quality improvements in social services due to slow economic growth.

Turning to another possible explanation of the success of social policies in the high achievers, an argument could be made that a major reason for their success was their relatively small size in terms of territory or population. That smallness provided an optimal context is moot. While this argument is indeed valid for two of the cases which are island states (Barbados and Mauritius), it is hardly valid for the remaining countries. Large populations are not typical for developing countries: there are no more than fifteen developing countries with populations larger than 50 million. The population size of the selected countries exhibits considerable range and is comparable to the population of most other countries in their region. Korea has 45 million people, and Malaysia 20 million; only Indonesia has a population in the East Asia region which is significantly larger than Korea. In South Asia, the relevant comparison is not with countries per se, but with states within countries which usually have similar populations. Kerala (30 million) and Sri Lanka (18 million) have populations comparable to those in the states of India and Pakistan. In fact, the argument of small size would hardly hold water when countries like China or Vietnam are taken into account; there are other countries in the same region with similar populations which could not begin to match the social achievements of those two states.[11]

A final point: could it be argued that ethnic homogeneity is a necessary condition for the potential of the state to follow polices which promote human development? It has been argued, for instance, that one reason why Botswana was able successfully to pursue human development policies was that, more than any other country in Africa, it is dominated by one ethnic group, the Batswana. (Or that ethnic divisions are not an issue in Korea or Cuba.) However, the majority of countries among the high achievers had racially or linguistically mixed populations: Malaysia, Sri Lanka, Kerala (with its caste conflicts), Zimbabwe, Mauritius and Costa Rica. Clearly, conflicts between linguistic or racial groups is a complicating factor, but what these countries have demonstrated is that there are policy instruments at hand which facilitate a skilful handling of those conflicts.

The search for an optimal context for social success seems, from the analysis above, like a mirage. Social success in the high-achieving states was the result of the quality and the timing of social investment, as discussed very briefly at the beginning of this section. If we were merely asserting on the basis of these historical studies that social investment leads to social development, it would be tautological; it is the distinctive quality of this investment, differing so markedly from the vast majority of developing market economies, that accounts for the difference in outcomes.

REFLECTIONS ON THE REPLICABILITY OF GOOD PRACTICES

What is the potential for replication, what kind of general insights can be learned about processes taking place, and what does it take to transfer a specific good practice to another area? We suggest that economic growth is a necessary condition of *sustained* improvement in health and education indicators and in the quality of social services, but it is neither a necessary nor a sufficient condition for the 'take-off' in social development.

The harder issue to resolve is what kind of political system (as opposed to political commitment) is most conducive to the replication of these good practices. While 'voice' in the decision-making process is a prerequisite, the more difficult question is how that voice is articulated. Clearly, a democratic system alone is not sufficient, though we found that it was definitely helpful. That it is not sufficient becomes clear from a contrast in the social indicators between two states in India: West Bengal and Kerala. West Bengal does much worse in social indicators, despite a left front government for two decades, in a democratic system, while Kerala has alternated between Communist Party and Congress Party governments, and has done much better. But is competition in electoral politics then a prerequisite for the replication of the good practices of the high achievers? The nature of the states in Korea and Cuba would contradict such a hypothesis.

The experience with the emergence of democracy (of a parliamentary or presidential kind) in Latin America, Eastern Europe and the former Soviet Union, or Africa, over the last decade offers no hope whatsoever that it will be combined with greater human development. In many countries in these regions the emergence of democratic forms of government has coincided with more market-friendly policies, liberalization and attempts to integrate into the global economy. These trends have gone hand-in-hand with a historically unprecedented worsening in the distribution of income in many of these countries, combined with slow growth (in Latin America) or stagflation (in Eastern Europe and the FSU) or nearly zero growth (in Sub-Saharan Africa in per capita terms). The deregulation and liberalization may have created opportunities for corruption on a scale much bigger than was possible in an earlier period of development.

This contrast between the high achievers on the one hand, and these other states on the other, highlights the following. Unless competitive electoral politics is combined with at least a social democratic consensus, it is unlikely that human development – 'the enlargement of people's choices' – will be promoted. Where the emergence of democracy has gone hand-in-hand with orthodox, neo-liberal policies, the situation is fraught with risks of unprecedented corruption and a widening of the in-country gap between the rich and the poor.

The only general insight that we can safely draw is that the causes and driving forces behind social success were historical, and very specific to the country in question. The social forces that combined to produce the revolutionary changes within a matter of decades in these high achievers can be understood in a national context, but can hardly be replicated. Social forces cannot be conjured up, nor can any amount of social engineering help to create them. Only policies can be replicated. Hence a comparative study of policies, especially in a historical perspective, across success stories is an essential ingredient if good practices are to be first established and then replicated elsewhere.

CAN THE HISTORICAL APPROACH BE REPLICATED?

The historical approach adopted in the longitudinal studies must be replicated. There are a number of other countries whose experiences deserve to be examined in some detail. In the East Asian region, there are at least two other countries that offer interesting examples of remarkable evolution in their social indicators (Thailand and Indonesia) while dramatically reducing the incidence of income-poverty at the same time. There are two good reasons why the evolution of social indicators in those countries needs to be examined in a historical perspective. Indonesia is a large country; between 1965 and 1995 it managed to reduce the incidence of income-poverty from 60 to 15 per cent, while making not too dissimilar improvements in its social indicators. It may thus offer lessons for similarly large countries. Thailand was also able to improve social indicators while at the same time experiencing a dramatic worsening of its income distribution over three decades.[12]

A second reason why this historical analysis is necessary – before someone tries to rewrite this economic and social history in their own ideological mould[13] – is that increasingly we read the argument that integration into the global economy and openness is not only the route to income growth, it is also the route to social development. It is an interesting and open question why, for instance, certain countries (e.g. Taiwan, Korea and Japan) were able to combine openness with social development and improvement in the distribution of income, while others (e.g. Thailand) were able to combine economic growth with social development, but not an improvement in the distribution of income. It would be useful to examine if the worsening of the income distribution with rapid economic growth in the latter was, in recent years, the result of the relatively poor performance relative to its Asian competitors on social, especially education, indicators, i.e. the inability of the relatively poor to take advantage of the opportunities afforded by globalization.

Similarly, in South Asia, it would be interesting to understand the reasons for the remarkable recent success of certain states in India (e.g. Himachal Pradesh, Tamil Nadu) in improving social indicators, in contrast to the vast majority of the northern states. In the Middle East, Egypt offers an interesting case: despite not being an oil-rich state, it has succeeded in increasing life expectancy over 1970–97 from fifty-one years to over sixty-six years, reducing its IMR from 157 to 54, ensuring a net enrolment rate at primary level of 95 per cent and at secondary level of 75 per cent. It is important to examine cases in each geographic region, so that the case could be made both on a global and a region-specific basis for the replicability of best practice.

In fact, given how often a painstaking historical approach is substituted by cross-section analysis, with econometric analysis thrown in to strengthen what would otherwise be little more than ideological arguments, it is crucial to understand what would be a critical or threshold level for specific health and indicators before the *entire* population, rather than merely a small elite, begins to benefit from openness to the world market. For instance, for African countries, at primary enrolment rates of 20–30 per cent (in many West African countries), to diversify their exportables beyond primary commodities in the foreseeable future seems unfeasible. A skill base, deriving from a literate labour force, would be an essential ingredient for the diversification of exportables. On the other hand, the experience of Korea and Malaysia demonstrates that, *under certain conditions*, it is possible for economic growth based on openness and market-orientation to lead to poverty reduction and social development. It is necessary that such historical analysis be devoted to addressing the complex question of the interaction between the policy instruments that can trigger the synergy between income growth, a better dispersion of that income, and health and education development (see Mehrotra and Delamonica, forthcoming).

It is unfortunate that, although there now exists a full half-century of experience in the post-colonial epoch of development strategies working and, for that matter, failing, not enough use is made of a historical approach to understanding the issues that could be helpful to policy-makers currently engaged in formulating development strategy.[14] Part of the reason is that historical research requires the availability of data and, even more, the detailed, careful time-consuming mining of data. Where research is driven by international agencies on a limited time-frame, as is often the case, it does not help such an enterprise. Certainly, the study of the experience of the high-achieving countries demonstrates that such historical research is not only necessary and feasible, but can also yield useful insights.

NOTES

1. There are indeed such oil-rich countries where social indicators have not improved commensurately with expectations, e.g. Nigeria, Gabon and Venezuela.

2. Declaration of Alma Ata, International Conference on Primary Health Care, USSR, 1978.

3. The exception was smallpox vaccination, widely used in Europe from the late eighteenth century on, and the diphtheria anti-toxin discovered in 1894.

4. The level of spending is often determined by such unproductive expenditures as defence (which we found is low in the high achievers, by and large) and external debt servicing (which is of particular significance in the Highly Indebted Poor Countries, of which there are forty-one today).

5. This is one respect in which our conclusions differ from that of the Washington consensus. Leading researchers in the World Bank suggest that 'economic growth typically promote[s] human development, and a strong positive relationship is evident from the line of best fit (the "regression")'. It is acknowledged that there are deviations (the 'residuals') around this line; these are cases with unusually low, or unusually high, performance in human development at a given level of income or a given rate of economic growth (Ravallion 1997). They argue that the human development approach, espoused in the current chapter, devotes 'more attention to residuals' and the 'regression line is ignored'.

6. Botswana politics is indeed dominated by the Botswana Democratic Party which has won every election since 1964. The domination of the BDP seems to

reflect the popular will, in that it has consistently won an absolute majority of the vote. In a 1999 general election, however, the opposition parties made serious inroads into the BDP's parliamentary votes.

7. Over the 1980s and 1990s, this increasingly shifted to more bureaucratic forms of participation in response to central government policy. In 2000, the voting party held and lost a referendum on constitutional change.

8. A New Economic Policy was introduced after the race riots of 1969. The policy was based on a strategy of gradually redistributing wealth from growth rather than outright expropriation of the ethnic minorities. The indigenous Malay population, which predominantly lived in rural areas, was targeted to own at least 30 per cent of the corporate wealth (companies with shareholders funds above Malaysian Ringit 2.5 million were to allocate 30 per cent equity to Malays) and account for a similar proportion of modern-sector employment by 1990. To speed up Bumiputra participation in the commercial sector, the government set up state enterprises that provided employment opportunities at every level. Small and medium non-Bumiputra enterprises were basically unaffected by this law and left to grow (Leong and Tan 1997). The twenty-year time-frame, gradual approach and presence of escape routes for non-Bumiputra businesses helped to limit ethnic animosity towards the policy.

9. In Korea, early social development was driven by a military state (supported by the USA) facing a communist 'threat' from the north; once set in motion, the process was sustained by an authoritarian state committed to economic growth.

10. If countries like Laos and Cambodia did not achieve significant improvements in social indicators, for instance, a large part of the explanation must lie with the long-term effects of the war in Indo-China over two decades.

11. Similarly, Zimbabwe's population (10 million) is larger and Botswana's (1.4 million) smaller than that of the average African country. A small minority of African countries have a population exceeding 10 million (Nigeria, Ethiopia and South Africa among them). Among the Latin American cases, Costa Rica has a population similar to those found in Central America; Barbados is not very different from other Caribbean island states, and Cuba's population is that of a median population for countries in Latin America. Clearly, then, the answer to the question, Is a small population size a necessary condition for rapid improvement in health and education in a developing country? must be no.

12. Despite the increase in poverty in these two countries in the wake of the economic crisis post-1997, these and most other countries in the region were within a couple of years able to bounce back with positive economic growth – in strong contrast to the long recession that Latin America underwent after the debt crisis of the early 1980s, or Eastern Europe and the FSU during the transition to a market economy in the 1990s. This recent episode in their economic history in fact strengthens the case for an in-depth analysis, of a historical kind, of their social development.

13. The specific reference here is to the World Bank's *The East Asian Miracle* (1993) which was severely criticized by many independent academics, apart from the Japanese government.

14. For instance, in the late 1990s, there was a great deal of discussion of good practices in social policy that would be driven by a request by the G-7 to the World

Bank to propose such principles of social policy, especially suited to a context of economic crisis, e.g. in the wake of the Asian economic crisis (1997–99). The World Bank has gone about formulating such principles, essentially based on its own project experience. Such experience, while not inconsiderable, may not necessarily be the source of all the wisdom on the subject.

REFERENCES

Alailama, P. and N. Sanderatne (1997) 'Social Policies in a Slowly Growing Economy: Sri Lanka', in S. Mehrotra and R. Jolly (eds), *Development with a Human Face: Experiences in Social Achievement and Economic Growth* (Oxford: Clarendon Press).

Deininger, K. and L. Squire (1996) 'A New Data Set Measuring Income Inequality', *World Bank Economic Review*, Vol. 10, no. 3, pp. 565–91.

Duncan, T., K. Jefferis and P. Molutsi (1997) 'Botswana: Social Development in a Resource-rich Economy', in S. Mehrotra and R. Jolly (eds), *Development with a Human Face: Experiences in Social Achievement and Economic Growth* (Oxford: Clarendon Press).

Grootaert, C. and R. Kanbur (1994) *Child Labour: A Review*, background paper for the 1995 *World Development Report* (Washington DC, mimeo).

Krishnan, T. N. (1997) 'The Route to Social Development in Kerala: Social Intermediation and Public Action' in S. Mehrotra and R. Jolly (eds), *Development with a Human Face: Experiences in Social Achievement and Economic Growth* (Oxford: Clarendon Press).

Leong, C. H. and S. H. Tan (1997) 'Malaysia: Social Development, Poverty Reduction, and Economic Transformation', in S. Mehrotra and R. Jolly (eds), *Development with a Human Face: Experiences in Social Achievement and Economic Growth* (Oxford: Clarendon Press).

Loewenson, R. and M. Chisvo (1997) 'Rapid Social Transformation Despite Economic Adjustment and Slow Growth: The Experience of Zimbabwe', in S. Mehrotra and R. Jolly (eds), *Development with a Human Face: Experiences in Social Achievement and Economic Growth* (Oxford: Clarendon Press).

Mehrotra, S. and E. Delamonica (forthcoming) *Basic Services for All? Public Spending and the Social Dimensions of Poverty*, UNICEF.

Mehrotra, S. and R. Jolly (eds) (1997) *Development with a Human Face: Experiences in Social Achievement and Economic Growth* (Oxford: Clarendon Press).

Ravallion, M. (1997) 'Good and Bad Growth: The Human Development Reports', *World Development*, Vol. 25, no. 5, pp. 631–8.

Siddiqui, F. and H. A. Patrinos (1995) 'Child Labour Issues, Causes and Intervention', *Human Resources Development and Operations Policy*, Working Paper no. 56 (Washington DC: World Bank).

UNICEF (1993) *State of the World's Children* (New York: Oxford University Press).

World Bank (1995) *Sri Lanka Poverty Assessment* (Washington DC: World Bank).

FIVE

Best Practices in Poverty Reduction in Argentina: Towards the Identification of a Selection Method

ALBERTO CIMADAMORE, ERIKA VIDAL,
FABIANA M. WERTHEIN AND MICHEL
FLAMENT FULTOT

• The main purpose of studying best practices is to present and promote creative, successful and sustainable solutions to problems caused by poverty and social exclusion in order to build bridges between empirical research and the development of policies to reduce poverty.

A major challenge in this endeavour is to find a methodology to identify practices that would qualify as 'best' or 'good' among hundreds or thousands of these classes of events. It is imperative to answer questions such as: What could be considered as 'best' or 'good' practices on poverty reduction in an universe of practices carried out within a specific time and territorial framework? How can they be identified at a reasonable cost without being arbitrary?

This chapter outlines a methodology for the selection of best practices in poverty reduction, and examines two successful practices. In this way, it contributes to a first logical step before the necessary in-depth evaluation of the actual contents of a best practice.

THE SEARCH FOR A SELECTION METHOD

To identify a limited amount of good or 'best' practices implies selecting some and setting others aside out of hundreds or even thousands of poverty-reduction experiences. Such is the first challenge faced by researchers. The question that arises is how to handle this process as objectively as possible and to minimize the arbitrariness that appears along the way.

The first task faced by this approach is to limit the universe of potential best practices. It is reasonable to assume that a research project at a national level in a medium-sized country may deal with hundreds or even thousands of practices. A preliminary research conducted in Argentina indicated that the potential universe is large. In the public administration agencies alone there are at least fifty-nine national social programmes addressed to populations living in a situation of poverty or social vulnerability. Some of these programmes comprise several projects related to organizations that carry out anti-poverty projects, which considerably expands the universe to be considered. For instance, the Argentinian Social Farming Plan, between 1993 and 1999, supported 5394 different associative productive undertakings at the local level that could have been included in the universe of practices to be examined. Another example of the potential size of the universe is indicated in the number of NGOs related to poverty-reduction practices included in the database of the National Centre of Community Organization: 551 organizations targeting populations with unsatisfied basic needs.

Confronted with a potential universe that calls for a large-scale research project, it was necessary to adopt a second-best approach to identify candidates for the label of best or good practices.

This approach was based on the idea that administrators and scholars ('technicians') acting as an expert panel with a broad knowledge of these issues might be an important source for identifying the most appropriate candidates, once some well-defined selection criteria for a best practice had been developed.

The first step was to identify some of the principal experts in charge of large-scale programmes related to poverty reduction, as well as some of the major organizations and agencies working on poverty reduction at the local level. The next step was to interview co-ordinators of the different programmes and agencies in order to identify what they considered to be the two or three best poverty-reduction practices drawing on their experience and administrative knowledge, and according to the MOST criteria (see Table 5.1). Through this process a potential universe of hundreds of poverty-reduction practices was reduced to ten outstanding practices, an amount that could be handled by the scale of this research project.

Selection of criteria for a best practice   The selection of a best practice implies an evaluation, the criteria of which need to be made explicit.

Table 5.1 Criteria and operationalization of the criteria for a best practice according to MOST, technicians (administrators of the programmes and scholars), and beneficiaries of the programmes

MOST criteria	Operationalization of criteria
Innovation	The contribution of new and creative solutions to the poverty and exclusion problems
Sustainability	The viability over time of a poverty eradication practice, measured mainly through participants' involvement
Positive impact	Results which improve life conditions, quality and setting of the persons, groups or communities involved
Potential for replication	Potential to act as models to generate initiatives in other contexts
Technical criteria	
Efficacy	Achievement of the established goal through available resources
Efficiency	Effectiveness as related to cost
Management capital	Possibilities found to solve problems, find out about resources and access them as from knowledge gathered through experience
Organizational convergence among different actors	Establish relationships between the different logic and interests of participating actors

Positive change in expectancies	Growth of the expectancy level of a community, group or individuals who, without an intervention, would have given up their chances to improve their life conditions
Political viability in the local context	Establish co-operation and negotiation methods to deal with the political decision levels affecting the project
Political participation of beneficiaries	Beneficiaries give impulse, raise funds and establish social control mechanisms beyond their participation in planning and implementation
Beneficiaries' criteria	
Efficacy	Achievement of goals as perceived by beneficiaries according to their interests
Autonomous administration of the project	Decisive participation of the beneficiaries in the administration and execution of the practice/project (including decisions related to administration of funds and financial support)

Some of these criteria are already present in the decision-making involved in the administration and development of a programme.

It is important to incorporate different judgements – essentially originated in assumptions, norms and reference contexts (Briones 1985), that take into account different points of view from a diversity of actors (politicians, financing organizations, administrators, scholars and beneficiaries).

The analysis used in this research project acknowledges the existence of different points of view from which poverty-reduction practices can be evaluated. Therefore, the selection matrix proposed to identify best practices in Argentina includes three sets of criteria established by different actors.

The first set includes the general reference criteria established by MOST (the UNESCO research programme on Management of Social Transformations). The second set includes criteria developed by administrators in charge of poverty-reduction programmes in Argentina and a team of scholars working in this research (Technical Criteria). The third set includes criteria mentioned by beneficiaries of poverty-reduction programmes during evaluations of the practices (Beneficiaries Criteria).

The final selection of criteria for a best practice were based on the following assumptions. Subjective appraisals by administrators and experts are valuable because they come from people trained in evaluation processes and decision-making related to poverty reduction (Weis 1975). Administrators in charge of programmes behave based on a rational interest when they select those best practices that are somehow related to their programmes and agencies. Criteria that are agreed upon are more valuable. They turn the criteria into more robust reference data. What a beneficiary considers valuable is more useful and pertinent than theoretical criteria. Criteria are more reliable if they are related to an experienced situation.

Expert panel and selection of practices First, an overview of national databases on poverty-reducing programmes, projects and practices at a national, provincial and/or local level was undertaken. A selection of programmes with a poverty-reducing aim was done according to the following pattern: (i) that some sort of programme evaluation was already under way; (ii) that the programmes had a local basis; (iii) that they co-ordinated actions with NGOs; (iv) that evaluation records were completed by beneficiaries.

Second, administrators of the selected programmes were invited to participate in the selection process of best practices. An in-depth interview was performed with those project co-ordinators who responded to the invitation.

Then, a three-dimensional matrix was developed based on (i) the criteria established by MOST, (ii) the ones suggested by the interviewed administrators and the opinion of the team working in this research project, and (iii) those suggested by the programme beneficiaries' records.

Finally, an expert panel was called on to assess the relative importance of the different criteria of successful practices. It was composed of the administrators of outstanding anti-poverty programmes and scholars and technicians working on poverty reduction and methodology.[1]

The evaluation of the expert panel results went through a multi-criteria analysis and was further processed through the Analytic Hierarchical Process method.[2]

RESULTS OF THE EXPERT PANEL

As a result of this comprehensive selection process, ten programmes were identified as the best according to the three kinds of criteria developed for a best practice.

One of the methodological challenges was to determine the weight of each criterion with which to obtain a preference ranking of the projects in order to measure and compare the achievements of the best practices. For this task, a workshop was organized with a group of people responsible for social programmes and with the research team

Table 5.2 MOST criteria, results of the expert panel

MOST criteria	Order	Geometrical average	Final weighting	Minimum value	Maximum value
Positive impact	1	.433	.478	.200	.656
Sustainability	2	.291	.321	.100	.524
Replication potential	3	.106	.117	.037	.522
Innovation	4	.076	.084	.042	.203
Average inconsistency coefficient	—	.05	—	.02	.11

Table 5.3 Technical criteria, results of the expert panel

Technical criteria	Order	Geo-metrical average	Final weighting	Min. value	Max. value
Efficacy	1	.240	.289	.043	.445
Political participation of beneficiaries	2	.118	.142	.039	.318
Positive change in expectancies	3	.108	.131	.054	.279
Management capital	4	.097	.116	.036	.197
Organizational convergence	5	.093	.112	.030	.207
Efficiency	6	.091	.109	.022	.303
Political viability in the local context	7	.084	.101	.031	.187
Average inconsistency coefficient	—	.07	—	.03	.12

Table 5.4 MOST criteria, results of the research committee

Project	Positive impact .4780	Sustainability .3210	Replication potential .1170	Innovation .0840	Priority
P1.1	4	5	3	4	0.11882
P1.2	3	3	2	4	0.08386
P2.1	4	4	3	2	0.10500
P2.2	3	3	4	4	0.09047
P2.3	3	3	4	3	0.08810
P3.1	3	4	5	2	0.09810
P3.2	4	4	2	2	0.10169
P3.3	4	4	2	2	0.10169
P4.1	4	4	5	2	0.11161
P4.2	4	3	3	4	0.10067

Scale: 5 = Very High; 4 = High; 3 = Regular; 2 = Scarce; 1 = Null.

Table 5.5 Technical criteria, results of the committee of experts

Project	Efficacy .3858	Management capital .1549	Organizational convergence .1495	Positive change in expectancies .1749	Political viability .1348	Priority
P1.1	5	5	5	5	5	0.13382
P1.2	3	3	4	3	5	0.09151
P2.1	4	4	3	2	4	0.10938
P2.2	3	3	4	4	4	0.07990
P2.3	3	3	4	3	4	0.09205
P3.1	3	4	5	2	4	0.08458
P3.2	4	4	2	2	5	0.11066
P3.3	4	4	2	2	5	0.09437
P4.1	4	4	5	2	5	0.09437
P4.2	4	3	3	4	5	0.10938

Scale: 5 = Very High; 4 = High; 3 = Regular; 2 = Scarce; 1 = Null.

working in this project. They were invited to do pairwise comparisons of the practices to which the Analytic Hierarchical Process was applied. Thus a score was obtained for the criteria to be used in the selection process. Each expert determined individually the order of priority. Table 5.2 shows the geometric average of the assessments given by the panel of experts for the criteria developed by MOST.

This table shows two predominant attributes: impact of the social programme (43 per cent) and sustainability (29 per cent), which add to 72 per cent of the total relevance in order to identify eventual best practices. Except for two cases, all experts gave priority to these criteria.

The results from the expert panel's assessments of the criteria made by the administrators in charge of poverty-reducing programmes and the research team working in the project are displayed in Table 5.3.

The next phase aimed at selecting the final two best practices. This implied the rating and ordering of the ten projects selected initially, to obtain a preference ranking in terms of the criteria developed for a best practice. Such an approach allows choosing among the very best projects. The classifications were carried out separately for the two sets of criteria. The final order was built as weighted average of both partial scorings, assigning the same weight to the two families of criteria, and carried out by a research committee independent of the one that elaborated the initial weights of the criteria.[3]

Table 5.4 exhibits the partial scorings assigned by the committee and

Table 5.6 The final scores of each project

Projects	Final scoring
P1.1	0.12632
P1.2	0.08769
P2.1	0.10719
P2.2	0.08519
P2.3	0.09008
P3.1	0.09134
P3.2	0.10618
P3.3	0.09803
P4.1	0.10299
P4.2	0.10503

Table 5.7 Evaluation matrix for poverty-reduction practices

Success criteria	Selected poverty-reduction social programmes									
	Prog. 1		Prog. 2			Prog. 3			Prog. 4	
	1.1[1]	1.2	2.1[1]	2.2	2.3	3.1	3.2	3.3	4.1	4.2
Stage I										
Innovation*	4	4	2	4	3	2	2	2	2	4
Sustainability*	5	3	4	3	3	4	4	4	4	3
Positive impact*	4	3	4	3	3	3	4	4	4	4
Replication potential*	3	2	3	4	4	5	2	2	5	3
Efficacy**	5	3	5	3	3	3	4	4	4	5
Efficiency**	–	–	–	–	–	–	–	–	–	–
Management capital**	5	3	4	3	4	3	4	2	2	2
Organizational convergence among different actors**	5	4	2	2	4	2	4	2	2	2
Positive change in expectancies**	5	3	4	3	3	4	4	4	4	5
Political viability in the local context**	5	5	4	4	4	4	5	5	5	5
Political participation of beneficiaries**	–	–	–	–	–	–	–	–	–	–
Stage II[2]										
Efficacy***										
Autonomous administration of the project***										
Others										

* According to MOST programme ** According to technicians and administrators *** According to beneficiaries of projects/programmes

1. Selected practices: 1.1 Education and social integration in a poor neighbourhood in Bariloche, Virgen Misionera School Facilities, Province of Río Negro; 2.1 Production, packing and export by small-scale vegetable producers, Province of Mendoza. 2. Refers to the in-depth evaluation analysis stage that has not been completed at present.

Scale: 5 = Very High; 4 = High; 3 = Regular; 2 = Scarce; 1 = Null; – = without data.

the final priority of each project, according to the weighted average on each criterion.

As in the previous case, Table 5.5 exhibits the project's scorings assigned by the research committee on the technical criteria and the final priority.

The final order of the projects is obtained by means of a synthesis of the priorities of MOST and those obtained with the technical criteria, assigning to each family of criteria the same weighting (0.50).

The final scores of each project are calculated with: $\Sigma (x_i * 0.5)$, (x_i is the scoring of project i in each family of criteria). Priorities and the final score are given in Table 5.6.

THE FINAL SELECTION OF TWO BEST PRACTICES

According to the methodological guidelines previously described, two programmes were selected to qualify as best practices for poverty reduction at a local level in Argentina.

CASE I Education and social integration in a poor neighbourhood in Bariloche, Virgen Misionera School Facility, Río Negro

Objective The purpose of this project is to provide a poor neighbourhood with an educational facility which allows inhabitants to become integrated socially and workwise. Through education they can become skilled workers. And educational projects foster and consolidate positive change in the community's attitudes towards the poor.

Background The Virgen Misionera School Facility appeared as an initiative to establish a primary school for marginalized families. The neighbourhood is located south of the San Carlos de Bariloche city, and has a prior record of community work aimed at giving inhabitants advice and support regarding land possession. Family groups had settled on land owned by private proprietors, most of whom lived far away in Buenos Aires. Members of the team in charge of the facility realized the necessity to provide the settlement with school services that fitted the neighbourhood's specific needs and possibilities.

In 1983 the Virgen Misionera Primary School was created and soon initiated a remarkable expansion of educational activities within the community. In 1985 the Carlos Mugica Technical School was established to provide vocational skills for the workers, and primary and secondary school levels for adults were opened. In 1987 the facilities were enlarged with the opening of the Arco Iris Nursery School to cater to the needs of infants in the area. In 1989 the Amuyen Secondary School was created to provide courses that could facilitate poor people's access to the labour market.

The success of the project was partly due to the extraordinary commitment of the group responsible. The activities were self-initiated and progressively developed with financial resources obtained in different ways. Decision-making and activities were kept autonomous.

Characteristics of the undertaking The project consists of a series of school facilities developed as a 'public school with private management'. Formal education is provided along with informal education. Education for children goes hand-in-hand with education for adults. Inhabitants of other poor neighbourhoods and members of excluded social sectors living in the area also benefit from the project.

Religion has moulded the experience's leadership over time. The Río Negro bishop and the Neuquén diocese are committed to supporting the project.

The main institutional actors involved in the experience are: the bishop's delegate, who is the main person responsible for the project; the New People Foundation, an NGO in charge of legally ruling the project, constituted by some of its founding members; the committee in charge; teachers from the different educational institutions; administrative personnel.

Financial support is provided by municipal and provincial state means and international funding organizations. Teachers are paid by the provincial state, despite the fact that the school is privately managed. Dining-rooms receive financial support from the town council. UNICEF has supported informal training activities and technological resources.

The relationships established with institutions such as the Provincial Education Council have removed obstacles from the development of the project. Had these relationships not been developed, Virgen Misionera would have faced conflict with political powers capable of paralysing it or leaving it without essential economic support.

Evaluation of the project and its impact on the community The project has transcended the educational arena and become a crucially important tool for poverty reduction. The impact of the project can be observed in:

- Increased access to all educational levels (kindergarten, primary, secondary and even university) for a population which otherwise might never have completed primary school or would have deserted high school during the first years. It can be noted that twelve students who graduated at the Virgen Misionera educational facilities now attend university.
- Increased opportunity to become a skilled worker and improved chances of entering the labour market through professional training.
- Increased support for the regularization of the legal situation of land possession and eventual acquisition of land. The issue of land is part of the project's organizational mystique, as well as part of the group's daily practice of alternating school work with professional and personal support for the inhabitants.
- Increased family participation and mobilization of a co-operative spirit which gives synergy to the will to collaborate in project activities and fosters self-regulation and controlling skills in the community.
- Enhanced life conditions in general both for the people and communities involved.
- Increased positive change in the population's expectancies.
- Increased access to superior educational levels.
- Decreased violence inside the school facilities.

Innovation, sustainability and the potential for replication The project can be considered innovative because it involves the inhabitants in problem-solving and includes the beneficiaries and their surroundings' opinions as an evaluation tool. The Virgen Misionera facilities were created on the initiative of the area's inhabitants to solve the urgent problems posed by exclusion. As it developed progressively through financing resources obtained in different ways, it kept the autonomy of the inhabitants in decision-making and the activities.

The project has given the inhabitants a sense of achieving improvements within their environment for themselves and for future generations.

After more than fifteen years of operation, the ongoing expansion of the project and its ability to adapt to the political-institutional context attest to its high potential for sustainability.

The project can act as a model to generate similar initiatives in other contexts. Specifically, out of the results of Virgen Misionera a new experience was developed in another poor neighbourhood, 'the 34 hectares', where conditions are extremely precarious. Replication of the project seems to rest on the following conditions:

- A convergence of expectancies among beneficiaries, the project leaders and the local political authorities.
- The joint ethnic background of the beneficiaries and their appreciation of community initiatives.[4]
- A prior record of social commitment among those actors related to external powers (e.g. different levels of the Catholic Church, the municipal and provincial state).
- The local management capabilities, as expressed, for example, through the renewal of funding sources to achieve a variety of goals.
- The dissemination of the practice by those involved in the experience (authorities, administrators, university students from the neighbourhood, teachers, etc.), thereby generating social and political consensus regarding the value of the project.

CASE II Production, packing and export by small-scale vegetable producers, Mendoza

Objective The main purpose of this project was to increase access to local and regional markets, and even to export successfully, for a group of fifteen smallholding producers. Previously they had experienced great limitations to producing competitively, due both to the scarce availability of technology and capital, and to a low production yield. As a result their insertion in the market was marginal.

The basic idea was the fact that access to new production and markets is an important step towards the economic and social viability of smallholders. They need to enlarge their economic and social sustainability basis if they are to get out of exclusion and poverty.

Specific objectives of the project were to:

- bring technical knowledge about production and marketing to small producers
- increase participating producers' income
- improve sales strategies
- train producers to handle the production and marketing chain

Background Horticultural production is the main activity of the 6000–8000 small producers in the region. Their relationships with landowners and production means vary.

These small-scale producers face a series of limitations in order to produce competitively. Technology and capital are scarce, production yield is low, land and water are inappropriate, and market insertion is asymmetrical. Their resources consist mainly of their labour and the will to overcome limitations.

Encouraged by administrators from the National Institute of Farming Technology and the provincial government's Agrisol Programme, the smallholders contacted the Farming Social Plan in 1994. The first credit requested was devoted to individual work capital. When renewed in 1995, credit was used for the group's acquisition of machines and tools. Production of oregano was shifted to garlic, to benefit from competitive advantages in terms of profitability, price and market stability, as well as the product's resistance to weather contingencies.

After a while, most of the participating producers were able to produce garlic seeds for medium and large producers, an activity which allowed them to cover their credit obligations with the Farming Social Plan in advance.

Characteristics of the undertaking The project was developed between November 1997 and April 1998, in two stages: pre-investment and execution. The Social Farming Plan provided credits at a very low interest rate (an annual 4 per cent) compared with banks' credit rates (approximately between 12 and 14 per cent a year). An additional income allowed producers to plan ahead in order to survive and continue the productive cycle when they did not earn any money due to weather conditions or lack of temporary labour.

Producers who did not succeed with the initial project were allowed to return the machines to the programme in order to cancel their credit obligations. Machines were then reassigned.

The inner control systems developed by the group of smallholders, the close connection with the provincial co-ordination team and the team's autonomy in order to encourage project development contributed to making the necessary adjustments in the functioning of the programme.

The project focused on three dimensions: technological, economic and social-organizational. Pre-investments were given through funds standardized according to each activity. Special needs had their equivalent in the resources offered by the programme.

Actors responsible for the project were: the producers (beneficiaries), the area co-ordinator, the marketing contact person from the Social Farming Plan in Mendoza, the technician providing assistance to groups in the area, and the marketing agent.

Evaluation of the experience and its impact on the community The Social Farming Plan has an evaluation mechanism for best practices. Evaluation outcomes result from two annual evaluations of all the projects and from an external monitoring which uses the same basic indicators as regional evaluations, choosing a 20 per cent sample at random. Two specialists in social and production matters perform the external monitoring.

Evaluations indicate the following changes:

- positive impact on the producers' income as a result of the development of the project
- transfer and assimilation of management and organization capabilities to the producers
- incorporation of new technologies and knowledge in the production
- increase of innovative capacity among the producers
- use of planning and control as regular practices
- financial and book-keeping operations include the different actors involved (governmental and non-governmental)

More specifically, it was found that:

- produce was sold at a good price through channels other than the usual ones (individual sale at the ranch);
- producers with no prior experience in joint production and marketing, who had never worked on product conditioning, classification and packaging, managed to handle these procedures successfully;
- the necessary infrastructure was installed (a packaging warehouse) with an organizational scheme that guaranteed its adequate functioning, and provided work opportunities not only to the direct beneficiaries and their families, but also to other producers in the area;
- a marketing agent was hired in order effectively to co-ordinate and develop the planned actions, from choosing farming shares to collecting consignments' payment;
- producers participated in all aspects of the project. Handling and operation guidelines were developed in order to achieve better results;
- the experience confirmed the importance of the Social Farming Plan's

marketing guidelines such as: achievement of scale marketing economies; incorporation of added value to production; adequate use
of information regarding sales channels and buyers; development of
an adequate organization as the basis for success in each case;
- the project remained open for positive elements and aspects to be
improved in order to adapt the strategy to different productive contexts.

The following achievements were identified:[5]

- reduced production costs
- improved prices due to joint sales and purchases
- improved production process (technology, diversification, planning, volume and quality)
- the project contributed to keeping young people on the land
- improved self-consumption
- improved capitalization formation
- improved quality of life for the producers
- increased income
- creation of new work opportunities

Beneficiaries gave an overall positive appraisal of the project. Some
of the producers who received a subsidy offered in return to provide
services or perform other activities useful to their communities.

Innovation, sustainability and potential for replication The small-
scale producers' project was developed in a context with:

1. the prior existence of quite homogeneous social groups of producers
2. group members who share common life experiences and an organizational productive background
3. technical assistance and real demands stated by producers which were
well matched
4. technicians who were well prepared and familiar with the participants'
social and production conditions
5. an adequate integration between the different technical and political
decision-making levels (national, provincial and local)

The project's potential for replication depends on how the operational
components outlined above can be adapted to a new context. A crucial
question is how the producers can remain in that market when prices are

no longer favourable. Much would depend on the sales technique, acknowledging both producers' demands and context opportunities in a procedure which follows the sequence of production and marketing processes.

Transferring the Social Farming Plan practices is eased through the programmatic mechanism imposed by the producers' half-yearly meetings, in which critical and successful experiences are evaluated. Other means are the internships in which groups of producers and technicians from one area go to another to share their experiences. Valuable also is the dissemination of experiences through a series of publications distributed in different regions of the country.

CONCLUSIONS

The aim of this research project has been to identify and evaluate successful poverty-reduction practices at a local level through the design of a selection method that identifies the 'best' poverty-reduction experiences at a local level in Argentina. Hundreds of cases were turned into a limited field of study through a multi-actor, multi-criteria evaluation process. Two of the identified practices qualified as 'best' by fulfilling the requirements used in the selection and analysis process.

This work shows the need to use a best practice selection methodology that diminishes the arbitrariness of the selection process.

The selection of best practices can be considered a particular form of research evaluation of social programmes. In the same way as in the research evaluation, in the previous stages of selection it is necessary to use protocols that may guarantee the greatest objectivity in the judgements formulated by administrators, researchers and beneficiaries, considering the different objectives pursued by each practice.

The Analytical Hierarchical Process allows us to structure and to relate, from an agreed standpoint, different objectives and criteria coming from different actors or stockholders linked to the social programmes. The final grading of the projects can be obtained by means of the Saaty procedure (see note 2 below) or by other multi-criteria methods of aggregation. This chapter offers a first approach to the topic. Later on, the results obtained in this particular research may be improved through simultaneous application of three or four multi-criteria methods.

In the above-mentioned protocol, the importance of the judgements emitted by the beneficiaries must be stressed. It is necessary to deepen the analysis of the values and the beneficiaries' attitudes by means of improved in-depth surveys to obtain a coherent and substantive system of criteria that can be integrated into a wider system of evaluation.

The selection stage needs to be complemented by in-depth case studies of the practices identified in the matrix. This step should be directed towards assessing the conditions, attributes and features of practices that would be labelled as 'good' or 'best' in order to serve as a source of new ideas to develop poverty-reduction programmes and policies.

NOTES

We thank Else Øyen, Jona Rosenfeld, S. M. Miller and Atilio Boron for their helpful comments.

1. Expert panel participants: Atilio Boron, Alberto Cimadamore, Laura Golbert, Erika Vidal, Fabiana Werthein (CLACSO); Mónica Rosenfeld, Víctor Chevez (UNICEF); Gaston Bordelois (Programa Social Agropecuario); Ana Etchegaray (Fondo Participativo de Inversión Social); Irene Kit (Programa Social Educativo); Michel Fultot (multi-criteria analyst); Viviana Brenner (UNESCO).

2. The Analytic Hierarchical Process is a procedure delineated by the mathematician Thomas Saaty (1972). It allows a complex problem to be decomposed into different levels, the lowest with a bigger operational capacity. These different levels reflect particular aspects for the comprehension of the problem. Additionally, Saaty proposes a pairwise comparison method of each element of the lowest level with respect to each criterion to establish the relative global importance of the alternatives.

3. For the scoring of the projects the following verbal scale of preferences was applied (from bigger to smaller) in all the criteria: Very High, High, Regular, Scarce, Null. Then a utility function was determined assigning 5 for the best score (Very High) and 1 for the worst (Null) for all criteria. The expert choice software was used with rating applications in the ideal mode.

4. Part of the local beneficiaries' population comes from indigenous Mapuche ancestors, and Chilean migrants from the same origin. Therefore, it would be important to analyse this factor as the popular sector's social capital to face poverty-reduction practices.

5. 'Conclusiones del Encuentro de Pequeños Productores', Parque Norte, 11–12 June 1995, Buenos Aires, Argentina.

REFERENCES

Briones, G. (1985) 'Evaluación de programas sociales', *Teoría y Metodología de la Investigación Evaluativa* (Santiago, Chile: PIIE).

Cardarelli, G. and M. Rosenfeld (1998) 'Las participaciónes de la pobreza: Programas y proyectos sociales', *Tramas Sociales*, no. 2 (Buenos Aires: Ed. Paidós).

Castel, R. (1998) 'La lógica de la exclusión', in E. Bustelo and A. Minujin (eds), *Todos Entran. Propuesta para sociedades incluyentes* (Bogotá, Colombia: UNICEF/ Santillana).

Crozier, H. and E. Friedberg (1991) *El Actor y el Sistema* (Mexico: Ed. Alianza).

Golbert, L. and E. Tenti (1994) 'Poverty and Social Structure in Argentina: Outlook for the 1990s', *Democracy and Social Policy Series*, Working paper no. 6 (Notre Dame, IN: Notre Dame University, Helen Kellogg Institute for International Studies).

Grosh, M. E. (1993) 'Five Criteria for Choosing Among Poverty Programs', *Policy Research Working Papers*, no. 1201 (Washington DC: Policy Research Department, World Bank).

Grynspan Mayufis, R. (1995) *El concepto de Pobreza en América Latina y Estrategias para superarla*, III Simposio Latinoamericano Programas de Desarrollo Integral para la Infancia e contextos de Pobreza San José de Costa Rica.

Lo Vuolo, R. (1995) *Contra la exclusión. La propuesta del ingreso ciudadano* (Buenos Aires: Ed. Ciepp/Miño y Dávila).

Weis, C. H. (1975) *Investigación Evaluativa* (Mexico: Ed. Trillas).

SIX

Best Practices as Found on the Internet

JOACHIM HVOSLEF KRÜGER

• The concept of 'best practices' is found in many contexts, and poverty is but one of these contexts. Through the 1990s the number of publications and databases on so-called best practices (BP) has spread to include a range of fields and professions. Economics, business, industry, health, pedagogics, government, public services and management as well as the multilateral development organizations have incorporated the concept of BP. However, they give the concept very different meanings and put it to different use, from the simple exchange of success stories to advanced monitoring and the systematic collection and evaluation of practices.

This evolution of a new concept coincides with a decade of shifting paradigms in development theory on how to combat poverty. The dominant philosophy of macro-economics and structural adjustment as major tools to eradicate poverty and social exclusion now incorporates the building of human capital to enhance the human factor and its potential in the construction of more pro-poor communities. Thus, several major events, publications and summits have aimed at new agendas and global plans of action focusing on the human factor and local resources.[1] In particular the 1995 and 2000 UN World Social Summits on Development (WSSD) signalled these new agendas, but they were also catalysed by the World Bank and the United Nations' shift towards country assistance strategies.[2] Distribution of regional knowledge through global networking can likewise be seen as part of the new agenda. Projects move towards more knowledge-oriented poverty reduction and regional goals. The new indicators point to result-oriented local, national and regional strategies for poverty reduction. Therefore initiatives are taken to carry out local studies, collect and exchange data and promote more systematic use of indigenous knowledge. The development of a BP fits into this picture. Focus on thematic and regional interventions and transfer of knowledge are core features of the BP, and the Internet is a useful vehicle for discovering where and how success is to be found. In UN documents BP is presented as a central tool in development policy and anti-poverty strategies. Then it is launched, shaped and accelerated through the Internet. Consequently, databases are established with the purpose of mediating the projects and lessons learned from what are considered BP by the respective organizations, inside and outside the UN system. This process of exchange and generation of knowledge seems inextricably linked to and mutually reinforced by the policies of the main development organizations and the premises of the Internet. It runs parallel to the demands of access to information in today's globalizing world and the increasing demand for results and progressive ideas in politics. BP may therefore be seen as a phenomenon of the media and a symptom of politics.[3] A main feature of the Internet is its potential for 'mass-linkage'. As a result, creating BP-databases and linking them to other information networks can be seen as an incentive to create new programmes.[4] The outcome is, among others, a set of partially repetitive databases on BPs. At present it may be argued that their proliferation risks confusing rather than adding to the knowledge base of the original and sensible learning approach.

When analysing policies and trying to identify the visions guiding the different concepts of BP as a strategy, it is difficult to develop a clear picture of intentions and the framework in which the BPs are supposed to be successful. Concrete statements are hard to retrieve. Key source quotations and pronouncements of intentions flourish, while the concrete implementation of BPs remains remarkably unspecified on essential points. Words such as *traditional* or *indigenous knowledge* or *practices*, *good, effective, successful* and *best practices, solutions, success stories* or *policies* are often used interchangeably, and popular terms are not differentiated from political concepts and aspirations. The concepts and phrases mix easily due to their equally positive connotations and they promise results that inspire public confidence. Calling on social science is a re-emerging feature in the aspiration for co-operation between multilateral organizations earlier divided by boundaries in development philosophy.[5] Judging from this study, the level of precision has not improved along with the expansion of the BP databases during the last decade.

In sum, the quotations reveal a mixed use of terms and definitions related to the specific programmes, and the prefaces in BP databases hint at untapped resources and potential for new learning. At the same time, the vagueness of the approach seems a barrier to a learning that can create a successful implementation of the portrayed BP. The many links to other kinds of networking knowledge bases give a certain legitimacy to the usefulness of the BPs and the policies they promote. BP databases along with other knowledge-banks are directed towards the future generation of knowledge-based, legitimate policies. In this way they become also tools that validate strategies *in spe* and the policies they are to bear.

A GENERAL SEARCH FOR THE BP

If the Internet is to function as a medium for knowledge exchange, it depends on its strength as a public exposition room. During the last decade the Internet has become the main forum for publications on BP, mainly in easily accessible databases. The number of results delivered by search engines on the Internet on the phrase 'Best Practice' is overwhelming. Firms publish their BPs there, societies of professionals present their best results as BPs, public service projects present BPs as their main lines of guidance, and interest organizations display their favourite methods as BPs. The BP concept is promoted and recommended as a tool for improvement and a recipe for better performance, using the respective organizations or services as examples. The major development organizations follow the same pattern and their databases are among the largest and best profiled.

The searchable catalogues of major institutional libraries, though, contain relatively few pre-Internet publications on BP, and nearly all are from the 1990s.[6] The UNDP BP www-site started in December 2000, a sign of how new the use of this concept and its main medium still is.[7]

A search in the scientific library online catalogues ISI and BIBSYS shows, for example, that BPs in health and government appear under the heading of BP as a concept of evaluation or a transferable practice.[8] This is particularly true for economic issues. The phenomenon coincides with findings on trends in evaluation methods that take on economic management analysis such as Total Quality Management (TQM) and the Data Envelopment Analysis (DEA), or, in economics, 'frontier analysis'. The latter is directly connected with the term BP in a few titles, and the terms flourished side by side as evaluation methods in the late 1980s and 1990s. It is interesting to note that articles on BP do not appear in several major development economy journals such as the *Third World Quarterly*, *Third World Review* and *Journal of Development Economy*. Despite this, BP has entered the field of poverty reduction and social integration with great impact. It seems that exposure of BP is best done on the less demanding and formalized arena of the Internet where criteria of precision are not scrutinized by peer reviews.

WHO IS WHO? THE VISUAL RHETORIC OF THE BP-DATABASES

The general problems of Internet use follow the tracking of BPs as well. To identify sources, trace dates, sort out changes of content on a web-site over time, decide why and at what stage in history one database was linked with another, and make out who the different authors really are, are problems inherent in all database studies. In the present search, the same information and the same texts of explanation and presentation of BPs are found on different organizations' addresses, under different logos of sub-organizations, in different versions under the same programme, in partners' web-sites with links to related collections or to practices presented in other databases under different categories and designs. It is a jungle of words, created by the overwhelming number of links and size of online databases and characterized by endless and often altered repetitions. Thus, the origins of BPs as well as their organizations, programmes, databases and fields of concern are difficult to separate on the Internet. The multitude of links makes it difficult to see who are the mother institutions and who are the partners, and why certain links are established while others give only references to related web-sites. The information might be there, but the visual expression of multitude has a negative impact on the reading of a web-page's content.

The BP databases are linked to each other and the relevant organizations in most cases as if they share the same understanding of the BP concept, and why and how BPs are to be presented or implemented. A closer inspection shows the wide variety of BP contents and purposes. Databases may present selections or summaries of information on BPs presented in other knowledge-exchange databases. In this maze of information the major 'mushrooming' databases on BP thus may link BPs and other knowledge-resources of very different issues, criteria and aims. The reuse in BP databases of the case reports from so-called Indigenous Knowledge (IK) databases or knowledge networks indicates the tolerance for different contributors and perceives them as part of one general think-tank or knowledge-bank principle. Their successful practices are therefore integrated as BPs in other BP databases.

It seems to be an imperative for the general credibility of the holders of BP databases to expose the size of product and support it with a multitude of references and links.[9] In this way the large database-holders include visually several online resources as part of their own pro-gramme. This process towards a self-regenerating tendency of enlarging collections of links to resources related to the original programme by vague general ideas of knowledge-exchange does not increase the level of precision. It is difficult to know whether this entangled database-information on BP is the result of similarity in the information pre-sented, or rather highly different kinds of information linked under a seemingly uniform concept.

KNOWLEDGE-TOOLS: UNIFORMITY OR DIVERSITY?

Phrases such as *knowledge bank*, *think tank*, *global policy think-tank*, *knowledge-organization*, *knowledge creator*, *knowledge storehouse*, *knowledge disseminator*, *learning organization*, *knowledge base*, *information nexus*, *information super-highway* and so on can all be found in relation to the presentation of BP databases and linked knowledge resources. On the one hand, they are facets of an ideal of learning approaches, cf. 'know-ledge generation and knowledge sharing' in the words of the Global Development Network.[10] On the other hand, their idealistic coating adds to the legitimacy of the database-holders.[11] The vocabulary is used extensively in promoting organizations, their databases, policies and future goals. For the outsider it can be difficult, not to say impossible, to penetrate the actual meaning of the many words and to relate them to each other and to the concept of BP. They are brought forward as if there were consensus on their content. As this is not the case, the reader has to do his or her own interpretation. It is reasonable to assume that this lack of precision in the transfer of a BP to another sector or country is likely to hamper learning and knowledge production rather than enhance it.

The following list of major databases, organizations, programmes, quotations and use of terms, may give some guidance to the rhetoric and construction of BP projects and their attempt to tie into the wider context of the learning approach. Comments are included, and the italics are ours. This information about programmes, initiatives and organizations is found on several web-sites. Many web-addresses are given as guidance to the quoted documents or to relevant pages, and for the reader's own critical review.

BP PROGRAMMES, DATABASES, AWARDS AND LINKING RESOURCES[12]

The Best Practices and Local Leadership Programme (BLP) A 'global network of institutions dedicated to the identification and exchange of successful solutions for sustainable development. Contains learning tools, transfer methods, articles and other think pieces on what works.'

> www.sustainabledevelopment.org
> www.sustainabledevelopment.org/blp/blpmain.html
> www.sustainabledevelopment.org/blp/ or
> www.together.org/blp.html

'The success of the Best Practice Initiative for Habitat II has led to its incorporation within UNCHS (Habitat) as the Best Practices and Local Leadership Programme (BLP), a decentralized partnership programme that is comprised of leading research and capacity-building organizations around the world to continue the process of identifying, documenting and disseminating the lessons learned from Best Practices, and to monitoring the implementation of the Habitat Agenda.'

> www.cin.gov.cn/habitat/en/model/model01.html

'The Best Practices and Local Leadership Programme (BLP) of the United Nations Centre for Human Settlements (Habitat), is a global network of capacity-building organisations dedicated to sharing and applying the lessons learned from innovative practices. Together with the Urban Indicators Programme, the BLP forms the Global Urban Observatory, one of the principal means of monitoring and supporting the implementation of the Habitat Agenda and Agenda 21.'

> www.sustainabledevelopment.org/blp/aboutblp/

'[G]lobal co-ordination ... matching of supply with demand for information through: systematic monitoring and evaluation of trends and practices and the exchange of lessons learned; the development of new learning tools and transfer methodologies; informing policy makers at all levels; and, global dissemination through its home page, the Best Practices database, best practice case studies, transfer tools and methods.'

www.sustainabledevelopment.org/blp/aboutblp/

'[I]dentifying good examples of solutions to problems of human settlements and then effecting the transfer of those practices to places in need of such solutions.'

The centrepiece of the BLP is a database of 'Best Practices'.

www.together.org/blp.html

The 1996 UNCHS Habitat II Istanbul (section IVF) stated: '240. All partners of the Habitat Agenda ... should regularly monitor and evaluate their own performances ... and shelter indicators and documented *best practices*. The data collection and analysis capabilities of all these partners should be strengthened and assisted, where appropriate, at all levels, especially the local level. 241. ... Governments at all levels, including local authorities, should continue to identify and disseminate *best practices*.'[13]

'The ... way Habitat II contributes to good governance is by identifying and promoting examples of "best practices".'

Sustainable Development Organization   Refers to itself as an *information nexus for sustainable development*. It also monitors the BLP.

www.sustainabledevelopment.org

The BLP provides several award- and resource-links: as an extension of the learning-approach or idea of networking knowledge, the BLP 'seeks to establish close working ties with other Award systems and databases that share similar goals, principles and working methods'. The linked awards are: Local Initiatives Awards – ICLEI; Social Venture; Network Awards; Huairou Commission; CAIXA Municipal, Best Practices Awards; IFAD Desertification Award. BLP reason the linkages as follows: '[T]he BLP feels that users of such information are also entitled to know how *parallel databases and award systems complement each other in terms of the information being presented and how it is used.*'

www.sustainabledevelopment.org/blp/awards/other/

Best Practices Learning Centre '[D]edicated to improving public policy, management and governance through the sharing, exchange and transfer of knowledge.'

www.sustainabledevelopment.org/blp/learning/

'[T]o the maintenance of the Best Practices database as well as the Best Practices Intranet, a facility which allows partners and their network members to share, develop and exchange working tools on-line.'

'Lessons learned from, and transfer of, Best Practices. Guide to Transferring Effective Practices: A step-by-step approach to matching supply with demand for knowledge, expertise and experience in improving the living environment. Examples of successful transfers and lessons learned in Asia.'

www.sustainabledevelopment.org/blp/learning/learningmain.html
www.sustainabledevelopment.org/blp/partners/partnersmain.html

Best Practices Database on Improving the Living Environment 'Urban Problems Mushrooming First Ever Database of Urban Solutions Created'. This is certainly the most extensive and most complex database launching tools for implementation of BP. Its founders are: the Together Foundation, the United Nations Centre for Human Settlements/UNCHS (Habitat), Best Practices Partners and the governments of Spain, UK and Switzerland. UNCHS (Habitat) is also known as the UN City Agency.

www.together.org/
www.bestpractices.org/
www.sustainabledevelopment.org/
www.un.org/Conferences/habitat/unchs/press/bestpr.htm
www.bestpractices.org/cgi-bin/bp98.cgi?cmd=background

The Habitat Agenda (1996) and *BP initiative* gave birth to the *Habitat BP Database* 1996. Its BPs are launched for multiple criteria search, categorized in eighteen different areas of urban life development, with between four and nine sub-categories, following up Habitat programmes.[14] One category is *Poverty Eradication*. Each practice qualifies for three categories in search. Projects may as well be sorted under 8 *Ecosystem*, 8 *Scale* (*Village* to *Global*) or 6 *Geographic Region* categories. The database as well operates with Good, Best and Award winning Practices.

www.bestpractices.org/cgi-bin/bp98.cgi?cmd=habitat

Best Practices Database: Guide to Transferring Effective Practices A 'best practice transfer' in this guide further refines the peer-to-peer-learning concept and process ... a best practice transfer becomes both feasible and desirable when 'an organization recognizes that another organization has successfully implemented a solution for a set of problems or issues which the former is seeking to address and is willing to inspire its own actions based on lessons derived from that success'.[15]

Dubai International Award for Best Practices to Improve the Living Environment Established in 1995 by the Municipality of Dubai parallel to the call for BP by Habitat to create further incentives for producing applications for projects to be titled BP, 'Best Practices: Benefit for Humanity'.

> www.sustainabledevelopment.org/blp/awards/
> dubai-award.dm.gov.ae/
> www.sustainabledevelopment.org/blp/awards/
> www.hsd.ait.ac.th/bestprac/bpsubmission_2000.htm
> www.cin.gov.cn/habitat/en/model/model01.html

'[C]ommitment and willingness ... to share experiences is tangible evidence of the usefulness and validity of *the best practices approach* (m.u.) as a means of promoting the exchange and transfer of knowledge, expertise and experience in an increasingly interdependent and democratising world.'[16]

BLP Partners '[W]eb-sites of a global network of organisations and institutions devoted to applying lessons learned from experience to public policy, leadership and human resources development.'

> www.sustainabledevelopment.org/blp/links/

International Council for Local Environmental Initiatives (ICLEI) 'Among its other partnership initiatives, ICLEI has joined with UNCHS as a partner organization to the BLP. The BLP works with a decentralized network of organizations committed to the identification, analysis and dissemination of lessons learned from best practices.'

'ICLEI and the Habitat work together to gather, review, evaluate and disseminate best practices through this thematic centre focused on best practice initiatives of local authorities in the area of sustainable development and the environment.'

www.iclei.org/habitat-centre/index.htm
www.iclei.org/about.htm
www.iclei.org/iclei/bpsearch.htm

Best Practices Intranet '[F]acilitate networking, communication and information sharing. It forms the IT backbone of a knowledge and information management system ... used by the *Best Practices & Local Leadership Programme*, the *Ibero-American-Caribbean Forum on Best Practices*, the *Global Urban Observatory*, *Istanbul+5*, a joint Habitat/ESCWA working conference and the *Regional Office for Africa and Arab States of UNCHS (Habitat).*'

www.sustainabledevelopment.org/blp/intranet/

Best Practices Partner Network '[A] decentralized network of organisations committed to the identification, analysis and dissemination of lessons learned from Best Practices.'

www.sustainabledevelopment.org/blp/partners/

Ibero-American & Caribbean Forum on Best Practices

www.sustainabledevelopment.org/blp/partners/

Knowledge Management and Best Practices Links Page '[A]n annotated list of web-sites focusing on lessons learned from experience in making our cities and communities healthier, safer, more equitable and sustainable. They represent, to the best of our knowledge, organisations that are committed to the open sharing of information, tools and methods in support of: partnerships; participation; decentralisation and empowerment; networking and the use of information and communication technology.'

www.sustainabledevelopment.org/blp/links/

MOST Clearing House Best Practices database or MOST Clearing House Best Practices database on poverty and social exclusion

Successful projects related to poverty and social exclusion UNESCO's Management of Social Transformations Programme (MOST) database links BPs from other BP and IK databases on the subjects of poverty reduction and social exclusion. It consists of two BP main databases (see below), overviews and links to what are regarded as related BP and knowledge resources in a variety of fields. These are reached through the linked www-page 'Sites for Best Practices' at: www.unesco.org/most/bphome.htm or www.unesco.org/most/bpsites.htm and the linked www-page 'List of Indigenous Knowledge Resource Centres' at: www. unesco.org/most/bpiklist.htm

'The idea of a Best Practices Database is based on the observation that carefully documented case histories can provide excellent guidelines for policy making and planning of new projects ... build a bridge between empirical solutions, research and policy.'

'Calling these activities Best Practices is to suggest that they can and should be replicated, that ideas can and should be generated from them.'

MOST announces that its aim is to 'facilitate, at an international level, access to information about Best Practices and to establish contact ... collecting information from all parts of the world about a variety of projects, policies and strategies related to the eradication of poverty and the reduction of social exclusion.'

www.unesco.org/most/bphome.htm#1 and www.unesco.org/most/bphome.htm#2

1. *MOST Clearing House Best Practices: best practices on indigenous knowledge* '(CIRAN) in co-operation with MOST has established a Database of best practices on indigenous knowledge. This database is part of the MOST database of Best Practices, which concentrates on poverty alleviation, but as yet has not touched upon indigenous knowledge. It contains examples of successful projects illustrating the use of this type of knowledge in the development of cost-effective and sustainable survival strategies.'

www.unesco.org/most/bpindi.htm

The database is also called Register of Best Practices on Indigenous Knowledge and MOST/CIRAN Database, part of a CIRAN/MOST publication on IK best practices. NUFFIC-CIRAN Indigenous Knowledge database delivered the present twenty-seven practices and till now there have not been any supplements.

Search categories are: Africa, Asia, Europe, Latin America/Geographical Index/Thematic Index/Index of Institutions at: www.unesco.org/most/bpikreg.htm

2. *MOST Clearing House Best Practices: best practices for human settlements* Habitat BPs are presented here under MOST's logo, in a different (MOST's) visual design and other categories than in the Habitat BP database.

'All of the programme summaries are taken from the Best Practices Database compiled by UNCHS (Habitat) and with the support of the UNESCO-MOST Clearing House.'

'The summaries of selected good and best practices are included in the MOST Database because of their particular relevance to or impact on poverty eradication and on social cohesion.'

> www.unesco.org/most/bpunchs.htm
> www.unesco.org/most/bphome.htm
> www.unesco.org/most/bphome.htm#1

Representing the BPs related to poverty reduction and social exclusion, the MOST BP-homepage presents BPs from the Habitat database with four categories,[17] although seven appear when the base is entered, including the first four.[18]

UNDP Experiences and Good Practices

> www.undp.org/poverty/practices/

GENERAL KNOWLEDGE INITIATIVES AND IK NETWORKS

Evaluation Knowledge System (EKSYST) UN/IFAD 1997. Referred to as 'knowledge-organization, knowledge creator, knowledge storehouse, knowledge disseminator, "learning" organization'. Its evaluation findings are stored in a *computerized system*. These are categorized as 'Lessons Classified by Themes' and 'Lessons Listed by Region'. This *Knowledge centre, computerized knowledge base,* is 'culled from 461 projects undertaken since 1978. ...(Programs) need to be cross-fertilized' and 'has already helped similar projects in Ghana, India and Nicaragua to learn from each other'.[19]

> www.ifad.org/list_eval.asp
> www.ifad.org/evaluation/public_html/eksyst/doc/prj/index.htm

The Global Development Gateway (GDG) 'A portal on development, where users can find information, resources, and tools ... and contribute knowledge and experience. A platform to share material, to dialogue, and solve problems.' Sixty-three partners and contributors, universities and development organizations are linked here.

www.worldbank.org/gateway/

Global Development Network (GDN) and Award Aims at *knowledge generation and knowledge sharing* 'to help bridge the gap between the development of ideas and their practical implementation'. Financed by the WB since 1998.

www.gdnet.org/subpages/about.html

'[T]he GDN Awards build upon what is already the largest competition for development research and projects available today. Overall, these activities seek to promote advancement in knowledge creation and capacity building in developing countries.'

www.gdnet.org/subpages/events_global.html

Indigenous Knowledge Initiative WB, Africa Region: 'Indigenous knowledge can be preserved, transferred, or adopted and adapted elsewhere.'

www.worldbank.org/afr/ik/basic.htm#web_links_networks

'The vision of a truly global knowledge partnership can only be realized if the poor participate not only as users of but also as contributors to knowledge. The Global Knowledge Conference 97 (Toronto, June 97) emphasized the urgent need to learn, to preserve and to exchange knowledge embodied in successful local practices so that they could be replicated elsewhere and applied in the development process. Academic research has documented the role of IK systems in sub-Saharan Africa and especially in the lives of the poor.'

www.worldbank.org/afr/ik/backg.htm

This site announces, 'Key Players: CIRAN' and 'Key Resources for Indigenous Knowledge, Important Web Links: UNESCO-MOST', referring to the BP database of the latter.

www.worldbank.org/afr/ik/key.htm#Important

International Network for Development Information Exchange (IN-DIX) '[C]ollaborating with the Global Development Gateway on a pilot initiative called Integrated Development Activity Information (IDAI).'

www.indix.org

Knowledge Management Systems WB. Intends to 'provide operational staff with customized information ... and direct access to best practices from inside and outside the Bank ... ready access to a variety of information resources, including: (i) "help desks"; (ii) on-line databases of policy papers, best practice papers, electronic forums, terms-of-reference, profiles of staff and consultants, and links to external resources; (iii) a statistical database containing internal Bank data; (iv) a clearing house function for data available from other agencies; and (v) a knowledge base on the economic aspects of human development, including good practice of economic analyses in project development.'

www.worldbank.org/html/extpb/annrep97/human.htm

Knowledge Network for Poverty Reduction UN. 'UNDP, with its partners is continually exploring, through research and knowledge networking, the causes of poverty and effective strategies for poverty reduction.'

www.undp.org/poverty/initiatives/pgm.htm

The Global Knowledge Partnership (GKP) Promoted as a '*knowledge base*' GKP is a 'partnership of public, private and not-for-profit organizations ... sharing information, experiences and resources to promote broad access to, and effective use of, knowledge and information as tools of sustainable, equitable development'. The GKP emerged due to the Global Knowledge 97 conference, Knowledge for Development in the Information Age.

www.globalknowledge.org

IK ORGANIZATIONS AND DATABASES

Database of Indigenous Knowledge and Practices WB. 'A framework for development.'

www.worldbank.org/afr/ik/datab.htm
www.worldbank.org/afr/ik/ikrept.pdf

Centre for International Research and Advisory Networks (CIRAN)
A division of the *Netherlands Organisation for International Co-operation in Higher Education* (NUFFIC).

www.nuffic.nl/ciran/

Netherlands Organisation for International Co-operation in Higher Education (NUFFIC) 'Linking knowledge worldwide.' Provides access to thematically and geographically specialized indigenous knowledge collections/databases worldwide from 1989 and onwards aiming at transfer of practices. Also presents: 'Best practices in the field of Indigenous Knowledge, illustrations of the use of indigenous knowledge in cost-effective and sustainable survival strategies. A co-product with UNESCO.' This refers to the UNESCO-MOST BP database.

www.nuffic.nl/index-en.html
www.nuffic.nl/ik-pages/index.html
www.unesco.org/most/bpikreg.htm

The NUFFIC-CIRAN Indigenous Knowledge database has delivered twenty-seven selected BPs on Indigenous Knowledge to the MOST Clearing House BP Database, thus creating the joint MOST Clearing House BP on Indigenous Knowledge database (above). NUFFIC operates as 'a clearing house for the global exchange of information on IK by producing the *Indigenous Knowledge and Development Monitor* (IKDM)'.

www.unesco.org/most/bpikpub.htm

Indigenous Knowledge and Development Monitor (IKDM) '[A] journal that serves the international development community and all scientists who share a professional interest in indigenous knowledge systems and practices (IKSP).'
Its Monitor is produced by NUFFIC-CIRAN in co-operation with indigenous knowledge resource centres around the world.

www.nuffic.nl/ciran/ikdm/index.html

Indigenous Knowledge and Development Network 'The IK-network aims at the sharing of information among the various stakeholders in development and to contribute to the challenge of knowledge for development, which is to combine indigenous (local) knowledge with similar experiences from around the world, and with elements from the world of science and technology.'

www.nuffic.nl/ik-pages/ik-network.html

Co-operates, sharing IK, with the WB-GDG in its Global Development Program.

www.nuffic.nl/ik-pages/index.html and
www.worldbank.org/afr/ik/index.htm

APPENDIX

Some contributory examples: key-document statements and quotations pointing to the general change of approach in the developing of ideas, rhetoric and practices around the learning approach of the 1990s and 2000.

WB 1992: WB Policy Research Bulletin, Vol. 3, no. 3 'After decades of continuing progress in multilateral trade negotiations, regionalism is once again being viewed as a solution to the major international economic problems of our times. What's going on?'

WB 1992–96: A Proposal for a World Bank Group Strategy, Harnessing Information for Development, March 1996, Ch. 4, p. 5 '[B]rokering knowledge. The World Bank Group can use its knowledge of international resources to understand its clients' needs and to tap expertise worldwide to meet those needs ... The WBG is uniquely positioned to gather and disseminate best practices on topics such as: project design ... a paper was produced on best practices in integration of public financial management systems ... exploring new development frontiers.'

UNDP 1994–97: II. Profile (untitled) '[G]lobal and regional programmes are facilitating the exchange of best practices. In the context of the United Nations Special Initiative for Africa, one example of UNDP upstream support to governance is the Africa Governance Forum – a series of annual meetings for: building partnerships, through exchange of information on best practices.'

'11. Continuing to sharpen the profile while responding to the specific needs of a diverse range of countries will remain a challenge for UNDP, together with programme countries. Reviews of country cooperation frameworks, evaluations and dissemination of lessons learned and best practices will be important tools for managing this. While pursuing this approach, the overriding priority will be to produce results where it really matters – at the country level.'

www.undp.org/publications/anrep97/profile.htm

UN 1995: Our Creative Diversity. A Commitment to Pluralism. Report of the World Commission on Culture and Development, p. 70 'The challenge today, for nations committed to cultural pluralism and political democracy, is to develop a setting that ensures that development is integrative and that there are *best practice institutions* built on genuine commitment to being inclusive. This means respect for value systems, for *traditional knowledge* that indigenous people have of their society.'

UN 1995: Copenhagen Declaration, 1995: 17 and 27, Commitments 3(k), 9(n), 29(c) '(k) Foster international cooperation in macroeconomic policies, liberalization of trade and investment so as to promote sustained economic growth and the creation of employment, and *exchange experiences on successful policies* (m.u.) and programmes aimed at increasing employment and reducing unemployment ...

'(n) Support South–South cooperation, which can *take advantage of the experience of development countries that have overcome similar difficulties* ...

'(c) Strengthening international data collection and statistical systems to support countries in monitoring social development goals, and encouraging the expansion of international databases.'

ID21/WB 1998 'Knowledge can be a double-edged sword: if not widely shared, these same advances threaten to widen the gap between the world's rich and poor. The challenge is to put knowledge in the heart of development thinking. The World Bank's comparative advantage lies in its ability to draw lessons across countries and regions, and to bring global best practices to bear in meeting country-specific needs.'

WB/IMF 1999: PRSP-Operational Issues, p. 9 '[W]e are engaged in a process of learning-by-doing in which we will continue to be guided by country-experience as it evolves.'

IMF 1999: The Poverty Reduction and Growth Facility (PRFG)
II. Objectives of the New Strategy and the Fund's Role:
'[I]implications of the new strategy for the Fund's own lending ...
it begins by setting out what the new approach is trying to achieve ...
to ensure that PRGF-supported programs stem from, and are consistent
with, PRSPs, and are formulated in close coordination with the Bank.'

www.imf.org/external/np/pdr/prsp/poverty2.htm

BLP (Habitat) 1999: Madrid Declaration of Principles, 4 June '4. The idea
of documenting Best Practices is meant to enhance sharing among
communities to foster mutual capacity building in face to face exchanges,
peer learning, and transfer systems.'

www.imf.org/external/np/pdr/prsp/poverty2.htm

UNESCO 1999: World Social Science Report 'The social sciences are
well placed to explore the multiple interfaces between local and global
systems. They can help us rise above short-sighted approaches to
economic development. UNESCO is committed to promoting the development of the social sciences in order to maximize their potential
service for policy-makers and society at large.'

*WB 1999: Principles and Good Practice in Social Policy, April, pp. 10 and
12* 'The Bank's experience in poverty reduction points to the importance of an approach to development that gives as much weight to social
and structural issues as to macroeconomic and trade issues ...

'Ministers emphasized the importance of the Bank concentrating on
strengthening its support for member countries in translating broad
principles into practical country-specific results, based on the bank's
extensive operational role in promoting broad-based poverty-reducing
development experience of best-practice which should be an important
part of the Bank's contribution to the United Nations discussion of
principles.'

*UN WSSD 2000: Preparatory Committee for Special Session of the Gen-
eral Assembly on the Implementation of the Outcome of the WSSD,
Geneva, April, p. viii* '[T]o address the social impact of globalization
... they should consider the national conditions and particular needs of
different groups of countries. It is necessary to move away from "one-

size fits all" solutions by putting the collective experience of the United Nations system at the service of individual countries in their development efforts.'

UNESCO-MOST 'It may not be accidental that the growing interest in the potential contribution of indigenous knowledge to development is becoming manifest at a time when current development models have proven not too successful. Today, hundreds of millions of marginalized people all over the world are still being excluded from the mainstream of development. These people have not benefited from development efforts which have mostly been based on a top-down development model, with the maximization of productivity as its major target.'

www.unesco.org/most/bpikpub.htm

UNESCO 2000: UNESCO's Contribution to Poverty Eradication, Executive Board 159 EX/9, 22 March, p. 6f '3.4 UNESCO was endowed with the mandate to contribute to world peace by stimulating intellectual cooperation.

'3.5 ... Social analysis is a field where UNESCO has a comparative advantage, which needs to be fully harnessed, developed and reaffirmed ...

'3.7 The Organisation's intellectual role as an *international think-tank* on development and poverty eradication means that it must have the capacity to analyse the effectiveness of policies in its fields of competence; to conduct research into the nature of poverty and its measurement ...

'3.8 One example of an arena in which knowledge is required, is the issue of the prevailing types of poverty and the dynamics of impoverishment. A need in this area would be to conduct research that furthers understanding on the distinction between transient and chronic poverty.

'3.9 A second area concerns institutional and governance issues such as decentralisation, *also strongly propagated by the World Bank and the IMF in the 1990s, and that now is submitted to some clear caveats* ...

'3.10 A third example relates to the nature of poverty itself: concepts of poverty can be geographically, culturally and historically different.'

UN 2000 'As indicated by the new Information Age, information technology is becoming a primary vehicle for communication and access to information. The sharing of information has become an essential tool for developing societies ...'

www.un.org/Depts/eca/divis/rcid/news/ecanws4.htm

NOTES

1. For example, World Bank Group, *World Development Report 1990* (Washington DC: UNDP, 1990); UNDP, *Human Development Reports*, 1990–2000; UN Summits on Children (New York, 1990); Human Rights (Vienna, 1992) and Population (Cairo, 1994). Historical summaries: UNDP at www.undp.org/sl/Overview/an_overview.htm; World Bank/C. M. Robb, *Can the Poor Influence Policy?* (1999), ch. 1, at www.worldbank.org/html/extpb/canpoor.htm#Read; IFAD at www.ifad.org

UNDP, *Introducing the Organization*, September 1998, p. 13: 'Governing Council decision 90/34 (1990) asserts that UNDP: "should promote human development" and build national capacity ... technology transfer and adaption; technical cooperation among developing countries ... In decision 95/23 (1995) the Executive Board adopts new, performance oriented arrangements for the distribution of UNDP resources.'

2. For example, UN, *New Agenda for Development in Africa*; *Strategy for Poverty Alleviation* (Gambia, 1990); UN, *Bangladesh Participatory Poverty Study* (1996); World Bank: *Assistance Strategies to Reduce Poverty* (Washington DC: World Bank, 1991); the *HIPC-initiative* at: www.worldbank.org/hipc/

WB Poverty Strategy www-pages: 'Based on the studies of many countries, cross-country analytical work and current best practice in development assistance, and consultations with other international organizations and NGO representatives, a framework has been developed that would help strengthen poverty reduction strategies in developing countries ... The key principles underlying the framework are that poverty reduction strategies should be country-driven, oriented to achieving concrete results in terms of poverty reduction.' At: www.worldbank.org/poverty/strategies/overview.htm

'[P]articipation of civil society in the adoption and monitoring of the poverty reduction strategy tailored to country circumstances will enhance its sustained implementation.' At: www.worldbank.org/poverty/strategies/principl.htm

WB Indigenous Knowledge Initiative, 1998: 'There is, therefore, a need not only to help bring global knowledge to the developing countries, but also to learn about indigenous knowledge (IK) from these countries, paying particular attention to the knowledge base of the poor.' At: www.worldbank.org/afr/ik/ikrept/pdf

3. Kofi Annan announced on 13 September 1997: 'The global agenda has never been so varied, so pressing or so complex. It demands of the international community new approaches, new resources and new commitments of political will ... In recent years, UNDP has worked hard at reinventing itself.' At www.undp.org/sl/Overview/an_overview.htm

UNDP, Management Development and Governance Division, Section II (http://magnet.undp.org/about_up/Mdgdbro.htm): 'Building on the activities of the Management Development Programme, started in 1989, the Management

Development and Governance Division was established in 1995 *to respond to increasing demands on UNDP* ... The Bureau captures and disseminates country-based experiences and best practices as a way of continually creating new knowledge and feeding back lessons' (our italics).

4. For example, UNCHS-Habitat BLP and Best Practice Database; UNDP Experiences and Good Practices, www-site; UNESCO-MOST Best Practice Database; WB Indigenous Knowledge Initiative (addresses: see list).

5. This is accentuated in UN, *What We Have Achieved* (Geneva: UN, WSSD-Declaration, 2000, p. 2), Commitment 10: §8 and 9: '8. Universities and policy think-tanks would be invited to create a volunteer corps of advisors to assist countries with such expertise as they might require. 9. Development research and policy networks, such as the Global Development Network (GDN) would be invited to help create knowledge banks and web sites to facilitate access to relevant experiences and knowledge ... UNDP's Netaid and other web sites of UN system agencies, notably those of UNICEF, UNESCO, and WHO could be linked to an emerging world-wide knowledge bank on poverty reduction. National and local branches of such a knowledge bank could form part of the poverty reduction strategies of individual countries so as to ensure that *indigenous knowledge* is brought to full bear [sic]' (our italics).

6. Online libraries searched via US Congress Library for this study, keyword 'Best Practice': US Congress Library; Australian National University; Commonwealth Scientific and Industrial Research Organization (CSIRO); Duke University Library; Earth Sciences Information Centre, Ottawa, Canada (INNOPAC); Griffith University; Kings College London; London School of Economics; New York University Library. At: lcweb.loc.gov/z3950/gateway.html#lc

7. UNDP at: www.undp.org/poverty/practices/

8. Institute for Scientific Information (ISI) searched via the University of Bergen Online Library Catalogue (BIBSYS) at: igate.bibsys.no/isearch/isi?lang=E

9. 'The Best Practices database: the world's most authoritative database on peer-reviewed good and best practices in sustainable development.' www.bestpractices. org

10. Sponsored by the World Bank since 1998. www.gdnet.org/subpages/aboutgdn.html

11. UNESCO, 'Contribution to Poverty Eradication', *Executive Board 159 EX/ 9* (22 March 2000) p. 5: 'The Organization's credibility and effectiveness in respect to development issues can be strengthened if it sets itself as an agency somewhat similar to a global policy think-tank.'

12. Some of the Internet links material here may have changed or become defunct.

13. www.undp.org/un/habitat/presskit/dpi1789e.htm

14. The Best Practices and Local Leadership Programme (BLP), Land Management Programme, Governance, Disaster Management Programme, Global Urban Observatory (Urban Indicators and Best Practices), Local Leadership and Management Training Programme, Safer Cities Programme, Sustainable Cities Programme, Urban Management Programme, Women and Habitat Programme.

15. BLP, BP Database: *Guide to Transferring Effective Practices. A Practical Manual for South–South Cooperation*, pp. viii f.

16. Dubai International Award for Best Practices, *Report of the Technical Advisory Committee* (5–8 June 2000).

17. Poverty Eradication, Social Exclusion/Integration, Urban Governance, Women and Gender Equality.

18. Three new categories are put on the website: Homelessness and Housing, Economic Development, Crime Prevention.

19. *Computerworld*, Vol. 31, no. 28 (1997), pp. 37–41.

Appendices

Acronyms and Abbreviations

AA	Alcoholics Anonymous
AL-ANON	Alcoholics Anonymous sponsor system
BDC	Botswana Democratic Party
BLP	Best Practices and Local Leadership Programme
CIRAN	Centre for International Research and Advisory Networks
CLACSO	Consejo Latinoamericano de Ciencias Sociales
CROP	Comparative Research Programme on Poverty
DEA	Data Envelopment Analysis
DFID	Department for International Development, UK
EAS	Employment Assurance Scheme, India
EGS	Employment Guarantee Scheme, State of Maharashtra, India
EKSYST	Evaluation Knowledge System
ESCWA	Economic and Social Commission for Western Asia
FINNIDA	Finnish Development Agency, Department of International Development Co-operation, Finland
FSU	Former Soviet Union
G-7	Group of Seven (wealthy nations)
GDN	Global Development Network
GDP	Gross Domestic Product
GER	Gross Enrolment Ratio
HDI	Human Development Index, UNDP
HIPC	Heavily Indebted Poor Countries
ICLEI	International Council for Local Environmental Initiatives
IDAI	Integral Development Activity Information
IDB	Inter-American Development Bank
IDS	Institute of Development Studies
IK	Indigenous Knowledge
IMR	Infant Mortality Rate
INDIX	International Network for Development Information Exchange

INTA	Instituto Nacional de Tecnologia Agropecuaria (National Institute of Farming Technology)
IRP	Institute for Research on Poverty, University of Wisconsin, USA
MIT	Massachusetts Institute of Technology, USA
MMR	Maternal Mortality Rate
MOST	Management of Social Transformations Programme, UNESCO
NGO	Non-governmental organization
NUFFIC	The Netherlands Organization for International Co-operation in Higher Education
OECD	Organization for Economic Co-operation and Development
PHC	Primary Health Care
PIIE	Programa Interdisciplinario de Investigaciones en Educacion, Chile
PRSP	Poverty Reduction Strategy Papers
TQM	Total Quality Management
U5MR	Under-five Mortality Rate
UIP	Urban Indicators Programme
UNCHS	United Nations Centre for Human Settlements (Habitat)
UNDP	United Nations Development Programme
UNESCO	United Nations Educational, Scientific and Cultural Organization
UNICEF	United Nations Children's Fund
USAID	US Agency for International Development
WB	World Bank
WHO	World Health Organization
WIDER	World Institute for Development Economics Research (United Nations University)
WSSD	World Summit for Social Development

About the Authors

ALBERTO CIMADAMORE has a PhD in International Relations from University of Southern California, Los Angeles, and a Master in International Relations from the Latin American School of Social Sciences, Argentina. He is currently Professor and Director of the Area of Specialization in International Relations, Master Program in Regional Integration Processes – MERCOSUR, Center for Advanced Studies, University of Buenos Aires, Argentina; Associate Professor of Theories of Regional Integration, Political Science Department, School of Social Sciences, UBA; Consultant on Trade and Regional Integration, Institute for Latin American and Caribbean Integration, Inter-American Development Bank, Buenos Aires; and Institutional Adviser of the Latin American Council of Social Sciences (CLACSO), Buenos Aires. He has published papers on negotiation analysis, regional integration and anti-drugs policy among other subjects.

MICHEL FLAMENT FULTOT is currently an independent consultant for the Inter-American Development Bank and is actively involved in applied research in social and health programes funded by the World Bank. He received his degree in Economics from University of Buenos Aires and has a minor degree in Industrial Management. He has held assistant and associate professorships at the University of Buenos Aires, the University of Salvador and University of Belgrano of Argentina. He has also lectured to international organizations such as UNESCO, the Regional Office for Science and Technology for Latin America and the Caribbean (ORCYT), the Latin American and Caribbean Institute for Economic and Social Planning (ILPES) and other multilateral agencies on topics such as multi-criteria methods, public investment programming and project selection and has also published articles on these topics.

ANURADHA JOSHI is a Fellow of the Institute of Development Studies at the University of Sussex, UK. She holds a doctorate in public policy from the Massachusetts Institute of Technology. Her research has focused on public sector performance and she has worked in natural resource management, anti-poverty policy and low-income housing. She is currently working on the politics and organization of anti-poverty programmes.

JOACHIM HVOSLEF KRÜGER is at present a student at the University of Bergen, Norway, studying for a Master's degree in History. He has a degree in History, Art History and Comparative Politics. In 2000–2001 he worked as an assistant at the Centre for International Poverty Research, CIP, and the Comparative Research Programme on Poverty, CROP.

SANTOSH MEHROTRA is a senior economist at UNICEF. Since September 1999 he has led UNICEF's research on social and economic policy in developing countries. He has studied at Jawaharlal Nehru University, New Delhi, has a Master's degree in Economics from the New School for Social Research, New York, and was awarded a PhD in Economics at the University of Cambridge in 1985. He was a Fellow at a government think-tank in New Delhi and taught Economics at Nehru University while consulting for UNCTAD and ILO, before moving to UNICEF, New York, in October 1991. His current research projects include public spending on basic social services, sub-contracted home-based work by women and children, the impact of the crisis on children in Indonesia, child labour, and financing of basic education. Mehrotra has written several books including: *African Economic Development: An Agenda for the Future* (1987, co-edited); *Development with a Human Face: Experiences in Social Achievement and Economic Growth* (1997); *Basic Services for All? Public Spending and the Social Dimensions of Poverty* (co-authored, forthcoming).

S. M. MILLER is director of the Project on Inequality and Poverty, at the Commonwealth Institute, Boston; former research professor of sociology at Boston College; co-founder and first president of the Research Committee on Poverty, Social Welfare and Social Policy, of the International Sociological Association; and is member of the board of directors of the Poverty and Race Research Action Council, United for a Fair Economy, and Social Policy, USA.

MICK MOORE is Professorial Fellow at the Institute of Development Studies at the University of Sussex, UK. His professional interests lie in the political and institutional aspects of economic policy and performance; the politics and administration of development, including anti-poverty policies; and markets and capitalism in developing countries. He has field research experience from Sri Lanka, Taiwan, Korea, India and Tunisia, and has extensive consultancy experience covering around twenty countries.

ELSE ØYEN is Professor of Social Policy at the University of Bergen, Norway. She is a past President of the International Social Science Council, past Chair of CROP, the Comparative Research Programme on Poverty, and is now Scientific Director of CROP. Her research interests vary from theory of the welfare state and comparative studies of social policy programmes in industrialized countries, to analyses of poverty phenomena in developed and developing countries and methodological issues in comparative studies. She has published more than a dozen books and several dozen articles within these areas. Øyen has been a visiting professor and has lectured widely at universities in many countries.

ERIKA VIDAL is a sociologist in charge of project evaluation at the National Institute of Indigenous Communities (INAI), Ministry of Social Development and Environment, Argentina. Currently, she is a graduate student in a Master's Programe in Social Policy at the University of Buenos Aires, conducting research in the field of indigenous cultures' potential for solving economic problems through their particular conception of nature.

FABIANA M. WERTHEIN has a Master's degree in international relations, from the Latin American School of Social Sciences, Argentina (1990), a degree in law, from the University of Havana, Cuba (1985), and a professional certificate in international trade, University of California, Los Angeles (1995). Since 1997 she has been an associate researcher, at the Research Institute, School of Social Sciences, University of Buenos Aires.

Participants in the Project

The following scholars participated in the CROP/ISSC/UNESCO/MOST workshop on 'Best Practices in Poverty Reduction' held in Amman, Jordan, 7 November 1999, and contributed to the discussion of the papers presented. Their many valuable contributions are gratefully acknowledged.

Ayman AbdulMajid, Birzeit University, Palestine

Arnon Bar-On, University of Botswana, Gaborone, Botswana

Abderrezak Benhabib, University of Tlemcen, Algeria

Madeline Berma, Universiti Kebangsaan Malaysia, Selangor, Malaysia

Erhard Berner, Institute of Social Studies, The Hague, The Netherlands

Einar Braathen, Norwegian Institute of Urban and Regional Research (NIBR), Oslo, Norway

Alberto Cimadamore, Latin American Council of Social Sciences (CLACSO), Buenos Aires, Argentina

Murat Cizakca, Bogazici University, Istanbul, Turkey

Constantine P. Danopoulos, San Jose University, USA

Blandine Destremau, Centre Français d'Etudes Yemenites (CFEY), San'a, Yemen

Atta El-Battahani, University of Khartoum, Sudan

Penny Johnson, Birzeit University, Palestine

Anuradha Joshi, Massachusetts Institute of Technology (MIT), Cambridge, MA, USA

Nazneen Kanji, International Institute of the Environment and Development (IIED), London, UK

Kaylan Sankar Mandal, Indian Institute of Management, Calcutta, India

S. M. Miller, The Commonwealth Institute, Cambridge, MA, USA

Zulridah Mohd Noor, Universiti Kebangsaan Malaysia, Selangor, Malaysia

Shanta Pandey, George Warren Brown School of Social Work, St Louis, USA

Roberta C. Rivers, University of Botswana, Gaborone, Botswana

Nader Said, Birzeit University, Palestine

Tokiko Sato, Japan International Cooperation Agency (JICA), Tokyo (observer)

Mohammad Shafi, Aligarh Muslim University, India

Faridah Shahadan, Universiti Kebangsaan Malaysia, Selangor, Malaysia

Hassan Shawareb, The Jordanian Hashemite Fund for Human Development (JOHUD), Amman, Jordan (observer)

Karori Singh, University of Rajasthan, Jaipur, India

Roni Strier, Involvement Center for Social Change, Jerusalem, Israel

Fayiz Suyyagh, Ministry of Social Development, National Aid Fund, Amman, Jordan

Khaled Tarawneh, Ministry of Planning, Amman, Jordan (observer)

Tahar Ziani, University of Tlemcen, Algeria

Index

ZED TITLES ON POVERTY

Many Zed Books titles on international and Third World issues deal, one way or another, with the question of poverty. The following titles, however, deal with the question specifically.

Aldrich and Sandhu (eds), *Housing the Urban Poor: A Guide to Policy and Practice in the South*

Siddharth Dube, *In the Land of Poverty: Memoirs of an Indian Family, 1947–97*

Lars Engberg-Pedersen and Neil Webster (eds), *In the Name of the Poor: ContestingPolitical Space for Poverty Reduction*

David Gordon and Paul Spicker (eds), *The International Glossary on Poverty*

Rajni Kothari, *Poverty: Human Consciousness and the Amnesia of Development*

John Madeley, *Big Business, Poor Peoples: The Impact of Transnational Corporations on the World's Poor*

Suzanne Thorbek, *Gender and Slum Culture in Urban Asia*

Willem Van Genugten and Camillo Perez-Bustillo (eds), *The Poverty of Rights: Human Rights and the Eradication of Poverty*

Francis Wilson et al. (eds), *Poverty Reduction: What Role for the State in Today's Globalized Economy?*

For full details of this list and Zed's other subject and general catalogues, please write to: The Marketing Department, Zed Books, 7 Cynthia Street, London NI 9JF, UK or e-mail:

sales@zedbooks.demon.co.uk

Visit our website at: http://www.zedbooks.demon.co.uk